I0236685

GRAYBEARD ABBEY

Also by Gavin Dillard:

Nocturnal Omissions [with Eric Norris]

A Day for a Lay

In the Flesh—undressing for success

Between the Cracks

Yellow Snow

The Naked Poet

Pagan Love Songs

Waiting for the Virgin

Notes from a Marriage

Rosie Emissions

Twenty Nineteen Poems

POEMS FROM
GRAYBEARD
A·B·B·E·Y

metaphors, mumblings, and meditations

by

GAVIN GEOFFREY DILLARD

GAVIN DILLARD POETRY LIBRARY & ARCHIVE
Black Mountain, NC

www.GavinDillard.org

Copyright © 2017 Gavin Dillard Poetry Library & Archive

All rights reserved. No part of this book may be reproduced or transmitted in any form or by any means without permission in writing from the publisher, except by a reviewer, who may quote brief passages.

Cover photo of Gavin Dillard by Parker J. Pfister

Book design by John Marcum

First Edition

ISBN: 978-0-9982887-0-3

This book is **dedicated** to *Felis catus,*

with infinite **gratitude** to Professors Tom Kellie and
Philip F. Clark for their patience, support, and editorial eyes;
and to John Marcum and David Dalton for their patience,
brilliant design skills and technical support.

My sincere **apologies** for not having a proper index of titles and
first lines, but, really, it would end up half the size of the book
itself. Thus, I would advise the reader to mark favorites,
turn down pages, or insert kitty whiskers as required.

Herein are the complete poetic journals of 2016,
penned at **Graybeard Abbey** in Black Mountain, NC.

GRAYBEARD ABBEY

Gavin Geoffrey Dillard

2016

Five quilts on the bed and I
still feel the warmth of the
kitties above—
outside, the moon cracks the ice on the
pond; winter has finally arrived.

Cold night—the fire embers wink and
pop—one avoids stepping on
naked floor boards;
I wrestle with cats and bedding until
only my hair is exposed.

No crickets no cicadas no
frogs chirruping in this
deadly cold night.

Siamese cat at the foot of my
bed, keeping an eye out for
monsters—
allows me to
dream without worry.

Outside, a world of ice,
inside, a world of firelight and
happy kitties;

on a night such as this, one cannot
help but send out a prayer of
warmth for all creatures that
live in the woods.

When life itself becomes
hallowed, candles and
incense, statues and
bouquets, both lose and
acquire their meaning.

Out of nothing and nowhere my
lover arises; within and without he
is, invisible he appears—
but do not ask his Name!

Neither mortal nor god, untouched he
caresses me, unmoved he
moves me, unknown he alone
knows me.

But do not ask his Name, for he is the
nameless who names all—
he answers only when I say
"Yes."

Poverty needs humility to
keep it company,
otherwise it's just another
misfortune, like wealth,
or fame.

Dogs bark on surrounding neighborhood
streets, a passioned dialectic in the
dark.

Some speak of existence, others argue
non-existence, and so they yap and
yammer until dawn—

such is the
nature of mind.

Some nights the fire won't
catch—same wood, same
paper, same kindling,
different night;

there are no answers in this
mortal life, only sparks that
occasionally and spontaneously
ignite.

Beyond the mists, above the clouds and
storm, the Moon shines effulgent and
profound—

she needn't be petitioned, nor
invoked,

merely gaze heavenward,
or into the dark pool of your
soul, and in her own good time,
         she will appear.

All things point to the
perfect Moon—but, in pointing, one
misses the point!

I meditated until I saw that I was the
object of my meditation;

I yearned for love until clarity
assured me that I was the source of
same;

I prayed to God until I realized that
God also prayed to me (now we
pray to each other);

I prune the roses now and know that
the Fragrance which arises is my
very soul.

Stepping into the water
the reflected moon
quietly dissolves.

If nakedness does not
come from within, it is
indeed obscene.

How easily my body fits into
yours, and yours into mine, my
Love, maker of my soul—
even the deluded wanderings of my
mind have not torn us apart.

A thousand times I have died in your
arms, my Love;
it has been a splendid, tempestuous
game—
but you always win!

When Love comes to bed, who wants to
sleep?
I sit up all night, listening to the
pattering rain, calling you by your
inaudible Name.

Life is messy, then we
die, and leave our friends to
sweep up the debris.

This world is cracked to me, and all its
contents spilled out.
I am tired of patching things up—
and so, step over the rift and
continue on my way.

Does the sea reside in the fish or the
fish in the sea?
does the mountain dwell in the tree or
the tree in the mountain?
I have lost such distinctions since the
Sky has taken up residence in my
heart.

This wee black kitten, she has
pilfered my heart—
and yet how innocent she appears!

How unsullied realization,
having abandoned thought;
how wide the Sky, once one's
stories become naught.

Even through layers of curtains, the
cold plummets down upon my
pillow; the warmth from the fire in the
front room never reaches my
bed—
the cats, however, meander back and
forth, shifting their allegiances from
fire to bed, ever seeking
Perfection.

I am infinitely more interested in
that which I cannot know than in
that which I can.

Does winter bring a promise of
spring, or merely the
eclipse of summer?
Sometimes the cold
is enough.

The fragrances of the earth enjoin and
blossom in my nostrils and
sinus—
breath is what we
share with the world.

I have no opinions that are
original—
but an open palm bears the
seed of fruit
hitherto undiscovered.

The Grim Reaper, not so
always grim,
beckons at times
with a
song and a grin.

Have we forgotten the gods, or have the
gods forgotten us?

Perhaps it's time we squash their
impotent representatives and
take back what is ours!

Half man, half God, we
stumble through the quagmire of
creation—enthralled by
pain, but ever
tethered to love.

There is a silence in the wind,
there is a silence in the rain,
there is silence in thunder; for in
their power, their command, their
certainty, nothing can be said—
one merely covers one's head and
bows.

There is a silence in the motions of the
clock, for in between seconds there is an
immortal stillness.

There is a silence in the heart, for
in between its compulsory, ritual
pulses, God dances unchained.

We do as much wrong to presume that
another soul might wish to
end up in our heaven as to
consign said soul to
our hell.

Infested with fleas and lice, my bed is
not the place it once was for
passion and romance—and yet, and
yet, who are these marvelous Beings with
candles, conch, and bells?

Sometimes giving something away is the
truest means to enjoy it—such is also
true of habits and addictions.

On such a frigid night,
even enemies are
tempted to spoon.

Winter's conundrum:
stay inside and watch the
embers go dark,
or brave the outside to
gather more wood.

Impregnating virgins to
beget demigods—
have the angels learned nothing?

In this temporal world,
even our shadows
succumb to darkness.

Having executed her
duties admirably, the
mantis lies dead on the path.

Fretting about salvation,
my mother lived a
life of hell.

The allure of the world has
fallen away, the dispiriting
rancour of civilization grown
fetid—nay, tedious.

When does love become absolute?
when does the ship sail for
Valinor?

O Śiva, blow my ashes from this
tiresome realm!

Ignorance is not fixed by
knowledge, but by true
simplicity—
the same is true of
knowledge.

Man hoists the assertion of
free will like a banner—
and yet, neither cloth, nor
pole or design
are his!

Form, appearance, knowledge, passion,
time, and fate are the six veils of
imaginary existence—
remove them and there is a nakedness
beyond nakedness.

Cold upon cold—
blossoms on the tea are
made of ice.

Age has many benefits, the prime being the
lessening of the yoke of desire;

young men and older women still find me
attractive—I'm more than contented with my
beloved felines:

In the dead of winter, a sunny day trumps any
parade that life might offer!

Poetry is something I was born with;
poem after poem, I had a bound book by
second grade.

I suppose I came by it honestly—unless one
considers stealing it from another
lifetime dishonest;

what now with my life? how long before this
chest of metaphors runs dry?

It is said that drinking enough
nettle tea will turn one's
skin bright blue—
O Śiva! will you
notice me then?

The flesh may be sagging, but the
pineal has been revived—
what I see now is more
enticing than the
candies of my youth.

I don't write poems to please the
gods, but only to appease my
soul; if a god is pleased, I am happy to
write him a paean—or happily lie with my
head on his feet.

I've never had a career,
I've never had a family;
  only poetry has sustained me—
and cats have given me
  someone to come home to.

Full moon on snow—
cold clarity.

The Self takes no pleasure,
the Self has no grief—
  how foreign Perfection appears!

Why replace religion with science? or
science with religion? both are false;
  miracles aren't meant to be understood—
the True Poet traces them back to
  their Origin.

Lost in the illusion, we
find our way—
  unlost, there *is* no way.

I cherish the intangible, for it
cannot be spoiled—and relish the
tangible because it can.

The Maryam statue in the grotto—
even more peaceful
draped in snow.

How gently the
leaves of the bamboo
cradle the snow ...

Hail then sleet then rain then
snow—
even the clouds are confused.

When the cat with the
smelly ass enters the room, the
other cats depart.

Frankincense oil cures
everything—
breathe deep my lonely heart!

With so many cats on the
bed, winter doesn't
stand a chance.

God is not separate from the
world and all its vagaries, and yet we
treat Him like a stranger.

A foot of snow—
even the full moon gets lost in these
endless drifts.

Ignorance and superstition rule the
world—

how to be a source of light for this
darkening realm?

Tonight, I am a source of warmth for
five kitties.

That which is unnamable the poet names in
metaphors and wild descriptors—
before falling silent, his craft but a pathetic
flirtation.

The grievances of the body are not the
grievances of the soul—
Spirit watches both with quiet equanimity.

In a world of pain and loss, love
matters, and every moment
counts—
Joy has a habit of
missing appointments.

Most creatures won't survive long in a
box—
neither will Love.

Take my house, I'll live in the
woods;

take my friends, I'll make new
friends (who nest in the
leaves);

take my body—and where it rots
bloodroot will bloom.

Sometimes I wish that I believed in
God, so I could put a name to this
thousand-hand Lover.

What is this pain in my head?
I rub it with frankincense oil and watch
comets go whizzing by.

War after war, everyone bows to a
greedy god—
is there anyone without blame?

After 1600 years, pagans have
returned to the Temple of Zeus to
worship—
if only their emasculated gods would return to
smite the Christian usurpers!

In youth one desires to outlive all
one's friends—
in age one wishes one had not.

Shoveling all day, I've made
paths through the snow that lead to
paths through the snow.

The fact of the matter is that we all exist only as
metaphor—
and only the Poet knows the meaning.

Night after night I await my
Lover's lips—
darkness is just a deeper form of light.

I have little or no interest in
that which can be proved.

As the snow melts, so does the
moon—as the night
grows ever darker.

If one cannot love God, one cannot
love man;
if one cannot love man, one
cannot love God.

The fish and the ocean are one,
the sky and the birds are one;
distinctions may seem apparent, but the
Spirit is the same:

O Mystery!

Buried beneath sixty years worth of
frost—who will visit this
lonely mountain?

Roadside Buddha buried up to his
chin—perfectly at home in the
silent snow.

O Sweet Mystery! all of life is a
sacred dance, and You the
music; guide my steps, tune my
ears, and give me the words to
move mountains!

As snow melts and plops from the
roof, in the greenhouse
orchids bloom.

It is winter, but a fog as thick as
magic has awakened the
peepers in the woods;

the black pond waters are alive with
churning sperm, the day's rains have
erased last evening's snow,

and all one's dreams of spring have
impregnated the sky with
silly, giggling jewels.

Patiently waiting for
Love's cruel hand—
even joy vanishes in that
coal dark
smile.

I'm a gardener, there's
always a thorn in my
finger—and a
rose in my heart.
O Mādhava!

The daffodils have awakened,
only to meet destruction—
O fickle Sun!

Master love in this
foul world and it is
yours forever.

These old eyebrows are starting to
look more like wings—
what heaven shall we fly to next?

Something I've learned from
kitties: you never know what's
waiting behind a door!

The old man wipes his
nose on his hand, then
reaches out to shake mine.

Always remember:
even pain loves itself.

If there's a difference between
love and joy, it is
not worth mentioning.

Is it from being a Sagittarian that I
lust to wander? such that when autumn is
upon us, I long to be the leaf which
catches its flight over the fence and
into fields yet explored?

Winter has come and bellowed and
brayed—who might show her the
path away?

Winter is chillier for the
loves that summer kept.

Planting spring's
nettle seeds—
stung by the winds of winter.

Why does emptiness seem
tangible on this
night of the Dark Moon?

Had I relied on logic to feed me, my
life would have been a
  dry and tasteless thing.

Slowly chopping the downed
hickory tree into
  kindling, a woodpecker
shouts expletives from an
  adjacent tree.

Despite the lush warmth of the
fire in the front
  room, Simone braves my
freezing bedroom to
  keep me warm.

Having given up alcohol, for a
time, I find my mind remarkably
  scattered and dim-witted.

So unrepentantly cold,
one fears the night itself might
  shatter.

Who needs gods when one has the
judgment of cats?

The greedy wind blasts at my doors and
windows, as if the entirety of the
winter sky were not space enough.

In love was the world
born—why should it die any
differently?

He who deceives, deceives
himself—for who is ever
fooled by cowardice?

I have visited my own
grave and found it
lacking in interest.

Winter winds rock the
house, but only the
ghosts are alarmed.

The ways of the world are simple and
complex; all day at home stoking the fire, splitting
hickory stumps, tending the flocks …

On this, the coldest night of the year, every
blanket and towel in the house straddles my
bed; three kitties atop the pile hold it all in
place.

The body swims through the waves, but the
spirit finds peace in the deepest depths; the
mind travels wherever it will—it is not
long for this dusty world.

Fourteen degrees outside—at least the
winds have abated; from my bed I can see the
glow of the gas flame in the greenhouse.

Two far-away professors have finished editing
last year's manuscript, leaving my eyes free to
stare into the fire;

when this incense stick turns to
ash, so will have my thoughts.

One foot in this world and one
foot without—
balance requires discernment,
discernment a steady
heart.

This Joy, which has been since before the
beginning, comes easily of a quiet
evening—tea in hand, cats in
tow, the falling of a gentle
snow.

1.

Liquid ice seeps from the sky;
the bamboo is a cascading fountain of
glass, icicle stalactites trace the barren
limbs of the mimosa ...

When was this world ever hospitable?
Since Eden it has been one fucking
thing after another;
but for my furry companions, I would have
abandoned it long ago.

2.

Ice from the heavens: is the moon
melting?
With the path thus lit, the journey
begins—but where to?

From a brazier, I watch a cloud of
frankincense dancing upward only to
vanish into the nebulous dark.

I see no point in belief, all it does is
muddle what *is*—
the True Poet writes with blood and
sweat, to rejoice or denounce his words is
pointless.

This world will end, as all worlds
do—but the immutable fragrance of
love rises ever upward toward the heavens.

Who needs gods when one has cats?
I make my oblations hourly—and they,
like the gods of church and
temple, remain silent and
unmoved.

Winter reprieve, a brisk but sunny
day;
finally pruning the dormant roses and
carting away the thorns, the cats a
stampede of joyous activity …

Five years at Graybeard Abbey: stay in
one place long enough and your
tracks disappear;
remain still long enough and even your
shadow disappears.

Evening chores: putting drops in the
old monk's eyes, chopping meat for the
kitties, cooking up rice for the

chickens' breakfast, calibrating the
temperature in the greenhouse, piling up the
wood stove, choosing an aromatic oil for the

diffuser;
on the bed, with Nina and Simone, reading
Gensei and the *Dhammapada*—what

dreams can I have but the union of
Saints, the joy of kitties, and the
blessings of poetry.

I am That. That I am.

Economy is a cancer. I was born a
poet and thus immune. Money has always
found me, but rarely through any
planning or contriving of my own.

And though habitually impoverished, I've
always had too much to eat, more
clothes than I can wear, and have fed my
cats the butcher's best cuts.

Economy is a cancer—a sham of greed and
crowd control; I look forward to being
ashes in a forgotten garden.

Like ink on vellum, one's thoughts of
God—apparently meaningful, until the
library is set ablaze.

Such a browbeating, these wrens—
remind me to never again run out of
bird food!

Few saints walk the streets of this
small town—of those out
walking their dogs, it's
usually to the dogs that I
bow.

A man with a well-fed cat on his
bed has
no cause to complain.

Clarity brightens the night—this
symphony of rain has structure and
purpose; three purring kitties speak of
comfort and security.
How can I serve through poetry?
—by being unattached to the
results.

Cured of my affliction, no amount of
gratitude is sufficient—
we are all absorbed into the Sun.

I *am* this solitary frog calling out in the
darkness, not for love, not for
companionship—
but because I love this crazy crazy
rain!

Humans were born to love; all
beings were born thus.
If love is not brimming in your
heart, you simply aren't
paying attention.

If I cut my hair and beard I could look half
civilized—but for whom?

The cats like me a tangle; I'm too old and
crabby to get laid; and the people I most

admire all lived long ago in mountains far
wilder than these.

Yes, I spent the afternoon beating up
God—to no great avail, I must
say.

We've made up now—he's letting me
 braid his beard; and there's something in this
wine he's poured that's making me feel all ...

mellow.

Heaven exists not in the
sky, but in the heart—
 stop looking and let it
find you: in all ways to
quietness yield.

Such a stunning creature, this
snowshoe, Shikibu, preening diligently upon our
bed; what an honor to provide sustenance and
comfort to such a regal beast!

In such a pairing as we, it is impossible to
discern who is guru, who is disciple, who the
lover, who the beloved;

I see no less God no less spirit no less soul in
 her infinite cerulean eyes than I do in
beings twenty times her size.

And I marvel at her noble presence which
always always coolly states,
 "*I am Cat I am!*"

Chrysanthemum tea and a sleeping
kitten—outside, the blustering snow is a
universe away.

Who can explain this madness, when planets
meet, revolve around each other, then
spin off toward the Sun?

Only the truly free can understand the
relationship between space and
gravity—

although I have to admit that anything can
happen when the Moon gets
tangled in your hair ...

O Immortal Self, grant me simplicity,
grant me humility, grant me clarity;

let the waters of life run clear and
clean, and the dust of creation go the
way of all dreams.

—*O Shining One, my Heart, my
only Joy!*

The markings of age on my face remind
me how valuable is the time I have
left—
the youth that I feel, a reminder of
that which lives on!

Experience is grace,
love is life;
only the lost find home.

True Love takes no prisoners, it is the
Ocean in which all lovers drown;
did you think it would be
easy, scavenging for life amidst the
dead and dying?

Leave the fundamentalists to their
fear and sanctimoniousness—their
drinks of choice;

come, get lost in the orchard with the
disciples of unknowing—get drunk on the
wine of Mystery and forget all you have

thought to be true.

What can I do? talking to burning bushes is
getting old! Enough with words, precepts,

laws, I want to fall into the fire where there is
no question of meaning.

No more stagnant stone tablets or one-
through-tens, God,

let's reduce this world to ash and
rise like the Phoenix to Penglai!

There is a special place in hell reserved for
people who lay claim to
God's name.

For the love of a cat great men become
greater.

There is no such thing as objective
reality.
If you want truth, you must tread beyond
reality, beyond science, religion, and the
senses.
Find a tree somewhere. Climb it. Fall.
That is your answer.

Form and formlessness are both
dreams of the dreamer, relative and
transient, like life—like death.

An afternoon in the woods, hands full of
thorns, hair filled with the
fragrance of leaves and twigs—
exhausted kitties—in my dreams I am
far off the path.

When the peony is
ready to sprout,
winter weather be damned.

What is it thinking, this
bamboo which blooms in
the snow?

No matter what my heart says, my
mustache keeps smiling.

A spring day in winter, ideal for planting
roses and chestnut trees;
  the cats peed on each one, I peed on each
one, and then dusted them with
  ashes and charcoal from last night's
fire.

Physical form is a mirage, as spirit is
mirage—
  but the fragrance of spring dives deep into
the heart of that which is
  Absolute.

It's not fair, those who leave us too
soon, like snow falling on
  ground warm with sun—
gone in a trice—and yet
  spring doesn't come!

I read my poems aloud—
the kitties yawn.

A smattering of snow on the
deck, kitty prints heading in
  both directions—
what is unavoidable, we surely
  must endure.

A sparkle of frost on the
weeping gingko, a
fountain of ice—
where are my thoughts when I
need them?

Voting day, we all line up, fools in the
snow—awaiting seasons
already destined.

Neither seeking nor desiring, the
Moon illumines this dark and
frigid world.

With a zillion stars to hold my
hand—what joy is
empty space!

When the Kundalini rises, there's
no use holding onto your
hat—with your
head still attached, it will
roam the galaxies.

Shaman kitty
stalking the shadows
for spirit mice.

As our democracy has crumbled, the
charlatans have arisen—
or is it the other way around?

Truth requires no reward,
for it alone is the prize.

At play all afternoon in the back
orchard; cats on patrol, hawks keeping a
lookout on high—
Spring is a temptress, showing but the
first glimpse of flesh.

Today buds,
tomorrow plum blossoms …
where will this madness end!

Teetering in the top of the hickory nut
tree, chainsaw in hand, a mile from the
ground—
one tiny bird comes to kick my
ass.

Frankincense in the brazier, the fragrant
smoke candescent in candlelight;
intoxication has many
forms—are there any that I've
missed?

Spring: did I hear it, Graybeard
Mountain yawning and
stretching?

When ecstasy blooms, even the
cherry trees take notice.

In the heart of man, forgotten,
the seed of magnanimity.

A visit from Father James—
the sharing of moscato and
heresies.

Worlds collide, often
unnoticed, as
universes keep expanding.

Past midnight, I mumble and
scribble, unmoved by either
desire or intention—
unslaked by
success or failure.

The pruned branches from the
peach trees—blooming where they've
landed in the orchard grass.

Here on the feet of Graybeard
Mountain, we care for cats and
chickens, bunnies and old
monks, and wander lost in the same
three acres day after day.

This wee kitten, Fledermaus, flitting from
chair to chair, loves to
snuggle; disturb her and she
bites, ignore her and she
purrs—
reminds me of so many past
loves ...

Such bad bad children, wandering the
streets, stirring up the dust looking for
God:

hold still for one moment, let the world
pass you by and just notice for the first
time who you really are.

Stop winding the clock, it will naturally
wind down, and time will be no
more:

Can you imagine a world without
you in it?
Good, I thought not—

now stay right there!

In this world of endless grief,
the cherry blossoms open
for five happy days.

I confess, I am a rotten gardener: I am
much more interested in what grows in the
woods.

Forget the neat little rows in the sun: I like
surprises—mushrooms today the color of
curry powder, tiny purple leaves from the
swollen elderflower stalks;

the pond is filled with great jellyfish of
bullfrog eggs, and when spring finally
arrives there will be newts aplenty to
dance with!

Who has mettle or inclination for cultivating this
perfect, mad, exorbitant chaos of life?
Certainly not the one who perceives himself as
just another sprout in a tireless garden;

let spring be the wake-up call for the
million years you have slept.

All day I plant, prune and weed the back
orchard. No one visits there, just
me; but the cats adore the time in the
wild, me as their anchor as they venture up
trees, and into woods and return.

Fifty years from now it will be a marvelous
forest, a gathering place for fox and
bear—and though I will be gone, my
ash will sweeten the loam where violets and
orchids bloom.

Peach trees in bloom
but nary a bee awake to
greet them.

The first mosquito of spring—
always received with
mixed emotion.

Love shouldn't come as a
shock, but it always does—
until it alone becomes the
norm, the Mountain upon which
one stands.

Even poets need sleep,
if only to reverse the tides of the
day's prose.

A fire in the woods, the first of the
year, two visiting Magi, a bottle of
moscato, cats on every rock and
stump; the tempestuous trill of
awaking frogs,
and the winking eye of a moon behind a
battlement of clouds ...

Through poetry we are reconfigured to
something more plastic than
prose, more pliable than reason,
and more
plausible than science.

Curry leaf tea restores an old man's
hair, but adds nothing to his
thinning years.

Thunderous rain upon the cabin roof,
and yet my heart remains
calm in your hands.

In one moment of love is all
love included,
for love is absolute, the envy of
angels, the despair of the
archon, the joy of God and the
purpose of creation.

Such clarity of purpose dazzles the
senses and stupefies the mind—
daffodils in full flower.

Plums, cherries, apricots, peaches,
almonds, magnolias, daffodils, all in
flower—bees swagger about in a
Dionysian revelry—
the fields, the woods, the orchards abuzz and
aflutter; and where, I wonder, does my
heart fly off to now?

Military planes fly over the
orchard—have they any awareness of the
peace that they disturb?

Ritual:

When the prodigal cat comes
home, fresh chicken is
chopped (for her) and a cocktail
poured (for me).

Tears from the weeping
cherries fill the
pond to the brim.

Fledermaus, black plume of a
tail, always in the
mark of a question.

I shoved the broken tooth back into
place and it seems to have
reattached—
is my smile now
false?

Cold, starry night—
the peach trees, in full bloom, seem
lost, forlorn.

Embracing the spring woods, the
ooze of desire—and yet, and yet, the apparent
acceptance of what is.

Today I accidentally referred to my
statue of Mary as "Nancy"—
and she just smiled, unperturbed.

The contorted quince is in
bloom—
an amusement park for the bees.

Tadpoles and newts churn the
wee pond—a bee on a leaf
takes a ride.

The trillium is up and in
bloom overnight—
if that doesn't wake the rest of the
forest, I don't know
what will.

Why does the full moon always seem like a
portal into another dimension?
—oh, that's right ... because it is!

Tonight,
incense so thick I can barely see my
own ghost.

Is the moon in the pond the
same as that which is
in the sky?

The medicine woman says that my body has
ceased aging—why didn't we think of this
thirty years ago!

Spring is always an anxious affair—
waiting for the cicadas to
tune up!

Hearing the geese but not seeing
them overhead makes me think perhaps I have
slipped into the wrong world.

The moon is a white lotus in a
midnight pond—her perfume
pervades the ethers.

Standing beneath the cherry tree, I
personally thank the bees for
attending to their blossoms.

My handsome and talented dentist keeps repairing my
broken teeth and I have quite lost track of
which are real and which not.

I have thrown everything at God that I could
possibly throw, and have found that it all
lands right back at my feet.

The tea trees are budding, there will be a
harvest in May, and the
ringing of bells at the Abbey.

Rosemary oil stimulates the
mind—but to what
avail, I wonder.

Daylight savings is useless,
our rooster has refused to
adjust his clock.

Already the tadpoles are gaining legs—
when I approach the pond, the gunshot of
tiny splashes ...

The tears of life are as passing as the
clouds beneath the moon—yet the moon remains
unmoved, smiling over all.

A sudden jolt of wind fostered a
storm of peach blossoms—
three kitties ran for cover.

In the violets by the stone Buddha,
rubbing a kitty's belly for
good luck.

Every day the peonies grow higher—
when they bloom the clocks will
stop and we will all stand agog.

A curry lunch with a bearded man,
an afternoon watering the gardens;
now, holy basil oil in the diffuser, cats
creating dreams for me to fall into—
O Allah! we dance until we stop!

Ostara weekend and everybody's potlucking and
cocktailing as they should be;
thank Goddess for my back fields, no one
comes there but the cats and I—and the
occasional murder of crows, carrying on and
        partying as they do!

In the diffuser, wintergreen and
sandalwood—
on my socks, lawn grass and chicken poop.

Barely spring and already the bugs are
biting—
what a tasty world we live in!

This peach tree with the
double blossoms really is a
pretentious bastard.

Izumi, the pied kitty, is
wearing a peach blossom for a
hat.

Soon it will end, this world of
superstition—
and then what will we believe in?

The Ocean is self-sufficient, and
yet it is fed by every
  spring and creek.
Why?
—because it likes the flavors.

I once was considered a great
beauty. Now snug beneath frosty
hair and beard; it is
not the years that make me old, but the
stories too numerous to recall.

Cherry petals sailing
downstream from an unknown
tree upstream.

Five weeks from Mother's Day, yet every
tree is blooming or leafing out—
are the gods of spring being kind or cruel?

In the pond's dark waters the koi
shift from sunny spot to sunny spot—
they know where best to dazzle!

It's always a bit sad when the
cherry trees fade—but in
360 days they will bloom again!

Too cold and I wake up shivering,
too warm and I wake up sweating—
the dial on this heater won't leave me alone.

Beneath the tree where
God sits,
a tiny throne made of ferns.

It is getting late and I have
written no poem—
how will I know I was here in the morning?

Everything we see is both revealed and
unrevealed. To see one way and not the
other is to miss the reality of
what is—
and what is not.

The peach blossoms are falling and there is
nothing to be done about it.
On the other hand, the fig tree is
leafing out, and Archimedes is sleeping
nose-to-butt in its half-shade.

Soon enough all my tattoos will
color a grave.

The old man in the front of the
house—I listen for his
final cough.

Confusion requires questions requiring
answers—
I prefer my questions unanswered.

Deafening, this chorus of spring
peepers around the pond,
   but only in my good ear—in my
"bad" ear I hear the hum of That which
has no seasons.

ME: So, God, what are my instructions?

GOD: How should I know, I haven't written them yet.

ME: Oh …

GOD: Just relax and follow the prompts, son, you'll be fine.

Afloat in this Sea of Jewels,
no paddle, no sail—
what would be the point?
—every moment an
ecstasy unlike any other.

Feathers in my bed—
two cats,
denying all charges.

Where consciousness blows,
love is the wind.

Sometimes dawn breaks at
midnight;
sometimes roses bloom in winter;
sometimes our heart
remembers who it is.

Why do I feel a greater kinship with the
newts, snakes, frogs, and turtles in my
pond than the hominids on the
avenue?

Perhaps because I too have made
peace with the mud and the
slime—

and remain entranced by every glimpse of a
celestial orb.

I spent two years staring at the
sun—now I am blind,
but can see Forever.

Why poetry?
Words cannot touch Source,
but metaphors can point the way.

I said to God, much before the
beginning of time, "Create me, and
I will sing and dance for your pleasure."

"*It's a secret,*" Gandalf said, "*keep it
hidden, keep it safe,*"
but I have stumbled, and love has
tumbled out of my clothing, my
pockets and my hair.

It is erotic, this Love, for it
touches every part of me, in a way that
no lover ever has.
That said, don't be shy, if you see anything
you like, come, pray with me!

When the technique can be
forgotten, the artist is free to
create;
when the religion can be forgot, the
soul is free to soar.

Don't be afraid of the dark,
sometimes God is modest ... as He
undresses you.

It's no use, avoiding Perfection—
it found you long before you started
fucking things up.

The pear trees are in
bloom—the nuanced scent of
semen.

I planted the bamboo over
there, now it is over *here*—
what an unruly child!

Spring came early, now it's being
fickle;
the trees look to me for help—
what can I do but
watch the leaves shiver?

This small-fry, Hafiz, will never
make it to alpha—in spite of a
healthy Napoleonic complex.

Weeping cherry
weeping blossoms—
reason to cry.

All we ever need is one moment away from
doubt to know that certainty is our
birthright.

I had a little purse of gold and silver coins, but
it has been stolen by a friend. There's a
lesson there: nothing is safe in this world of shadows.

When ecstasy comes upon me I retreat to
my room, the woods, the cellar or
barn; people get nervous when you
walk on water or float across the sky—
heck, even the sun gets jealous being
         outshone.

I used to have human lovers, but too
few of them
knew how to purr.

The funny thing about Source is that we are
always That; even those who wish to
take the long way home still end up at the
         Beginning.

Pain and suffering induce movement,
but it is joy that creates the greatest change.

"I am This, I am That ..."
—these crows in the yard aren't concerned
one way or the other.

What makes God so seductive?
Certainly not the lack of competition—
perhaps the fact that we have shared the
same bed since before there was
day or night.

Books are not holy, temples aren't
holy, religions aren't holy, for they
none contain the Spark of
Infinity that resides in the center of
every living being.

Thunderstorms in the middle of the
night—
tomorrow the peony will open.

I gave up love-making for Love.

There is no longer any question of
arousal—the entire exploding,
sweating, flaming, succulent, moaning,
writhing universe turns me on.

Please stop me if my incessant
kissing annoys you.

Well ... you can try.

Shameless,
a white peony in the
morning light.

Fledermaus curled against my
pillow,
chasing her dreams.

So many lonely widows, divorcees and
jilted lovers—
if only you understood how
excited God is to have your
undivided attention!

Every night I snuggle up with
God. And every night He says the
same thing: "Sing to me, my
Darling, and maybe, just maybe,
tonight you'll get lucky."

The great thing about Love is that it's not an
option, it's a mandate;

it was written into creation long before all this
genetic squirmy-wormy brouhaha, and it

requires no special instruction or equipment—
it's everything else that requires management!

And someday, when you're exhausted, when you're
completely wasted, you will fall into that

star and find the piece of sky that Love reserved
for you eons before time started acting like it

owned the damn place.

Wanting's a trip,
not-wanting is even more of a trip,
free will is downright laughable;
Perfection requires neither planning nor
tinkering.

Fearing God is like fearing your own
hand—like it's going to slap you or
poke your eyes out when you're not
paying attention.
We only fear that which we feel is
apart from us—
which God never is.

The only way to escape joy is to
pretend that something else matters.

Tangles in my hair, tangles in my
beard;
at last the vicious winds have
died down, restoring some
decorum to my thoughts.

Clarity. That's all that matters—
questionless, answerless, placeless,
timeless, faceless, nameless, non-doing,
not-non-doing, pristine clarity.
Bang.

God is always trying to
teach us his language—
but how few have the
ear for it!
   Shhhh!

Never ask "What is sacred?"
rather ask, "What is not?"
And if something does occur to you,
worship that thing until your very
soul becomes its supplicant.

The great thing about being round, the
earth once told me, is that you can
dance in any and every direction.

The animal self wants to be loved,
the spirit self wants to love;
but what about these tulips and
daffodils? do they bloom to love or to
be loved?
Me thinks they bloom out of
sheer joy!

In the darkest woods there is a
light of great clarity
shining on the creatures that
make the shadows their
home.

The concept of spontaneity
is not spontaneity.

I am less inclined to pray for what
isn't than I am for the
acceptance of what is.

The two angels at the gates of heaven and I are
old friends. We've argued in fact many
times—they have yet to let me pass.

Heaven is cruel that way, no one gets in until
they have finished living. But having
caught some glimpses of "the other side,"

I have lived faster than most, and always
kept my eye on the prize. Still, one wonders
what they're having for dinner tonight, in that

vast rainbow hall—and what darling there is
keeping my cloudly bed warm.

Theology—could there be anything more
tedious? It's like reading about making love.
Hell, it *is* reading about making love!

Because prosaic concepts are
contraindicative to God, the
poet uses his palate of metaphor to
describe what neither
is nor is not.

Waking this morning with a tick in my
neck and a tick on my arm—
this evening, the last fire of the season.

More and more I find myself
resenting the time I have to spend not
alone in the woods with the
kitties—where we needn't be
bothered by making sense.

The koi in the pond know that
it is spring—I can see them
smelling each blossom which
lands on the surface of their
universe.

This cuteness by my pillow—
every night she breaks the
heart that she heals.

Cancer is an easy fix—
meanness next to impossible.

When the cats come in
exhausted by evening, I know I've
had a good day!

Personally, I don't see much difference
between "right wing" and "left wing;"
Love on the other hand will always be the
most radical of politics—
let's roll with that!

A draught of Hendrick's makes the
absurdities of the day seem
reasonable, and the vagaries somehow
profound.

The fragrance of Love is never apart from the
flower of your heart;
but the stench of fear fills the streets and
alleys in this shadowy realm.

I suggest the woods and mountains for a
clear breath, and places where old
people, very young people, and animals
reside.

And, well, anyplace where
people are bleeding ...

If you want a religion, let it
be Nature,
for that's where God bathes.

A love like this cannot be
quantified. At one end it contains
all the known and unknown
universes—at the other end, one tiny
purring black kitten.

It's mid-April and already an itinerant
hummingbird—probably just passing through—
I hope she likes cherry blossoms!

Planting bamboo shoots up and
down the creek—
someday the deer will thank me!

I wear sorrow as an undergarment, beneath the
costumes of the day—viewed by only my
closest and dearest, but always
reminding me that this show of Life has a
final, irreversible bow.

Sleeping creatures, a silent
bed—no dreams will be
necessary tonight.

What do you know about God, someone
asked me. Oh, nothing really, I
said. Just what I've heard. And seen.
And of course smelled. And touched and
tasted. And that this Always Moment is
That and can never be anything other
than *That.* That's all.

I'm not a fan of science—
it's too much like religion.

Sick for a week and neither
eating nor bathing, tonight Simone
bounded in with a not-too-small
rabbit and proceeded to devour it all
over the kitchen floor.
Love is messy, indeed, but it is
always the cure.

In my back orchard, the surprising
Whorled pogonia orchids blooming amid
some rocks—such diminutive
specimens, one must get on one's
knees to worship them.

The trillium have ceased
blooming,
the *Iris cristata* are just opening—
to miss a day in the woods is to
miss a page of life.

Visiting with a friend in the Alzheimer's
house, I answered the same question
fourteen times—
how like all our lives this is, as endlessly
we ask God if he loves us.

A man of intelligence finds
distinctions—
the man of wisdom loses them.

In the back forty, *Isotria verticillata*, an
endangered terrestrial orchid which managed to
find me by letting me almost step on it;
what surprises and joys emerge from
sand—and a smattering of deer poop!

Staying up to the wee hours being
drunk with friends—when the full moon
rises, there's not a dry eye among us.

I love dead and fallen trees, they become a
home for so many humble creatures—
ferns and mushrooms find sanctuary, vines make
love to every knob and sinew;

I look forward someday to being a host to the
hungry and the lowly—what better way to
spread the Joy than to become the Feast!

The first warm night of
spring, doors left open, impassioned
crying coming from every
direction—foxes
looking for a fling.

Rescuing a snake from a
kitty's maw always seems
such a sacred task.

The bamboo I planted last week is
already sprouting—how long before the
deer pay tribute?

In the night breeze, the
thunder of a train—
but no rain.

Watering new plantings in the
woods—
a fat doe following closely behind.

Archimedes at the foot of our
bed, gazing out the
screen door, seeing things only
he can see. Some nights are
too beautiful for sleep.

To explore That which cannot be
known is the one passion which
cannot be outgrown.

The bridge between logic and
feeling all too often
sways in the wind.

Waiting for Love to rescue you is like
waiting for breath to breathe you—
simply inhale and embrace the Sky.

You will never find me fussing about
being awakened by thunder—it is
one of my favorite things, and a
language I understand.

Change can be traumatic, but it is
God's way of getting our
attention and saying, *Okay, enough of*
that shit, try some of this
shit.

Rain being one of my favorite things, it always
breaks my heart to have a body not conducive to
enjoying it fully—
next life I will opt to be a salamander, and the
puddles of the world my temples!

Thunder and lightning, a downspout from the
eaves, cats on the bed, hot curry tea, a
stack of books—
time has no sway here;
we are complete.

This pregnant deer, soon to have an
assistant to help her
devour my gardens ...

The marvelous thing about God—Truth, Presence,
Being—is that one doesn't have to
believe a thing. In fact, it only works when you
do not. But when one is There, one knows;
and when one knows, well, then you're
ever so blessèdly *There!*
So there.

To argue about *What Is*—a delightful
game! I play it sometimes, just to be
stupid. And then I have a
cocktail, and
shut the fuck up.

The roses have begun to bloom,
but all the cats see are the
butterflies!

This mosquito that bit my
third eye—did she steal rapturous visions,
or just blood?

Old age teaches one how few teeth are
needed for adequate dining, and
how few lovers for a proper night's sleep.

To the kitty that keeps bringing tree
frogs into the house:

Thank you, but I can
hear them just as well through the
screen door.

Most scientists, like most clergy, spend their
lives putting things into the appropriate
boxes—
but the great ones among us set the
boxes on fire.

Getting lost in the woods is my
delight, breathing the fog along the
creek opens the doors of
Mystery;

when that door is open, the voices
of the creatures who live there, the
language of snake and newt, dove and
crow, skunk and possum, all become a
vocabulary I have spoken since the

first mist formed into
sorrow and song.

I love reading books by dead
masters, but eventually their
words die too—and my
own pen wonders how long its
ink will last.

That which is Spirit cannot be known by the
mind, which is why intuition is the language of
the Divine;
through intuition one can know God in all its
eternal mystery.

And so we mature from instinct to intellect to
intuition, expanding and breaking boundaries and
limitation—to whatever is next, which can
not yet be imagined.
—*O Mystery!*

I planted a half-dozen sycamore trees today—
lovely trees, sycamores, artfully striated
bark, elegant nouveau leaves ...

In my mind I see the saplings, dug from a
gravel lot in town, already grown and
towering over the woods and creek; I may not

be here in 50 years, but it does encourage the
dears to get their root and leaf on when I
call them *Master, Goliath, Titan ...!*

Today I was reminded why stinging nettles are
called stinging nettles—it is never a bad thing to
reaffirm one's faith in language.

In the profound privacy of the woods, God lets
fall his robes and shows you what he's
been hiding.

Silence begets poetry and
poetry begets silence—
but genuine laughter surpasses both.

As this body has aged and
grayed, sensuality has become
deeper and without need.

Spring is a sweet anxiety,
awaiting the first cicada,
the first firefly ...

Hummingbirds!
Such flirts!

Our little pond is fed by no creek;
it never overflows, it never
diminishes—
what a magic home these
newts have!

All my life I've dealt with
crotchety old men—
finally I get to be one!

Tick in my arm pit, tick in my
hair—
this spring has become a blood fest!

Puzzled by the plush and fragrant cloud of a
peony flower, the hummingbird
hovers, flits away, returns, hovers, flits
away, returns, hovers ...
I cannot tell how this will end!

Awakened by the mating of
foxes at dawn—I do hope they have
found true love!

It is the duty of the poet to
live a life that others are
unable or unwilling to live.

Beautiful spring day—
the smell of something
dead in the shrubbery ...

What is the point of wanting stuff when you
realize you already have it all?
What is the purpose of grasping once you
understand that relaxing your grip takes the
prize?

It was when I became bored with the blood and
turmoil of war that Peace erased the
fear from my heart and the tears from my
face;

a gentle rain falls upon the bamboo and it
bows its head with complaisance.
On a night such as this, who can resist this
omniscient Silence?

When sleep comes, it is the
absence of dreams.

A friend reacted to one of my poems by
saying he treasured my work but did not
believe in God.

I explained that metaphors require no
belief—and he seemed satisfied.

Mind you, he thought I was speaking of
God, but I was actually referring to
him and me.

The pond in our woods is bottomless.

How do I know? I have wandered around the
edges in the soft silt attempting to weed the
banks, only to be sucked down and down to my
almost certain death. But more,

when the koi in the pond come up for air and
break the yellow-pollen surface I can see through the
black holes they make into a vast infinity;

but more, when the same koi poke through they
tell me of strange monsters and sea
creatures encountered in the depths—and on the
other side!

Agarttha resides beyond and within, and one
only need swallow one's disbelief to
awake there.

The antique roses bloom but
once in the spring—
the fragrance lasts all summer.

I am old, I cannot remember from one
moment to the next, but I can
remember every moment of my
childhood in which the
faeries tagged me to dance!

Who's to say that the beggar is not more at
peace than the billionaire?
I have been both, and yet cannot decide.

Perhaps we judge that which needn't be
judged because of guilt and desires we have
not reckoned with.

I look at it this way: Who is most apt to
see the Moon when she rises, and
watch her set,

and dance with her in the street or on the
mountain, unashamed, unabashed?

A bundle of peonies in a bucket,
pinker, plusher, and smellier than anything my
grandma ever wore to church.

Reality ...
now *there's* a concept!

Knowing as I do that everything I touch is
also God, and that everything I don't touch is
God as well, I remain free to touch or not
touch as my heart dictates, and ... well ...
I am free.

*[Note: Speaking of free, always feel free to
substitute the word Love for God, as you so
desire.]*

Because I love
I know I am.

True heresy is not renouncing God,
but rather reclaiming God from a
religion that has enchained Him.

Dragonflies in May—
always so proud of their
new wings!

I have never been particularly comfortable in this
body. That might be considered a problem by
some, but it has left me ever aware that there are
finer things in store for me once I have been
granted my parole.

Speech is like a baby, once birthed you
can't just stuff it back inside.

Of all my roses, the wild ones
smell the sweetest.

Poverty has been a
great ally in this
world of cheap excess.

Wealth can come and go, but
poverty stays true, once she has
been embraced.

Through Joy are all
things revealed—
nobody likes a sullen god.

Games sustain us in times of apathy and
ennui—
Hafiz stalks prey invisible even to the other cats.

Rituals sustain us in times of apathy and
ennui—
I light up a pipe unused for more than a year.

In a garden a million miles from
Vrindavan, I see Ananda Mayi Ma walking
among the roses.

Brugmansia flowers aggressively perfume the
greenhouse—the resident tree frog has
much to say about this!

The prayer flags on the cabin are
shredded and pale—perhaps it is time for
some new prayers.

Spreading chicken poop in the
rain—and still the
scent of rose and lilac.

After their dinner of diced
chicken, the cats are all
out chasing moonbugs.

Waiting for rains that never come,
tomorrow I'll spend with
buckets in my hands—
and live satori between
grunts and groans.

The monk in the barn gives
"loquacious" its meaning—
a proper thunderstorm might
shut him up.
Or not.

Up in the middle of the night sucking on
melatonin tablets, and black seed and
honey for a sore throat.
How patient the sleepy cats are with my
scribbling—
they know they'll never have to
read it.

The tide which laps the shore returns to its
Source again and again;
wander as we will, we are always ever Home.

The rain and the wind blew against the
spring flush of the roses—now the yard is
confettied as if the parade has just passed.

I used to have to look for words,
now they find *me*—
even when I'm hiding.

Why look outside of yourself,
there *is* no outside-of-yourself—
look to the Heart instead.

No time has passed since the first time I
fell in love, although an entire
creation has erupted.

Dancing all afternoon in the back
orchard, just I and three deer, four
kitties, and a dizzying, clamorous wind.

Like the tattoos on my aging
skin, so many things in life are
becoming less defined.

Love naturally begets Peace, for it
recognizes no conflict;
Love doesn't fix things, because it
recognizes no brokenness.
Only Love is—this cannot be challenged.

There are problems with drinking too
much, just as there are problems with
drinking too little.

I may be talking about booze here, or I
may be talking about water, or
lemonade—you decide.

Or perhaps this is all a metaphor for
blissful, ecstatic Union. In any
case, moderation is generally

called for—though I confess it has
never been my personal M.O.

—*Skål!*

Peony: extravagant, pompous, and
short-lived—
    the perfect weekend fling.

I couldn't possibly write another poem about
the peonies (at least not until *next*
    spring—except maybe for the burgundy
one, which just opened for the first
time, and which looks much like the
heart of a ruby, exploding into a
    supernova).

As I write, poetess Fledermaus nibbles the
fingers of my other hand. She's
    making a point about poetry, pain,
and blood—
    all the while purring.

Beauty, innocence, passion, the young
man wept to see our roses in full
flower—
    a thousand blooms this spring, and
    Enrique is one of them.

I *am* love. I *do* love. I *be* love.
So when the deer in the woods come up and
nuzzle against me, it is no surprise.

People are another story. They
run from love, and expect me to
chase them.

But I don't. And I won't.
Love waits patiently—
until the end of time.

New shoots on the timber bamboo nearly fifteen
feet high that weren't there mere days ago—
where on earth do they come from?

Why were the hawks shrieking at
dusk, sad to see the chickens file into
their hutch for the night?
—sometimes, often times, love has an
edge of danger.

I am babbling, but surely you
catch my drift:
words only fail because we
attempt to hold them to their
meaning.

Turn off the "news," shut the gates, and
sit beneath the maple tree; let a
  cat be your guide and squirrels your
guardians.

The movement of the clock is
just random opinion, the day is an
  endless moment; what we call "life" is a
succession of still moments.

Who's to care if a starling raises her
brood in your hair? if the ants create
  bridges into your soul?

What god would fuss if you acknowledged
  no "higher" power than the soughing of
your own breath in the breeze?

The cat has fallen asleep in your lap; the
sun has set in your eyes, and moonlight
  pours out of your throat like dragon's
milk.

Don't change a thing; there is nothing to
"heal" or "fix"—every second is
  precious and rare.

The more I desire solitude, the more
friends surround me—
  would it be rude to stop serving tea?

This house now is to be turned into the
Gavin Dillard Poetry Library and Archive—
and I, archived within its walls!

Loneliness I do not know, at least not in
any negative way—cats follow me about like
children heeling the Pied Piper.

There was a dead hen this morning.
Perhaps she is the one that had been
laying shell-less eggs—
something was awry:
I'm sorry I never named her.

I turn my back on the smiling
prophets of "abundance,"
little has always been enough for
me—and even that more than I can
carry in this floating world.

Sleepy cats beckon me to
bed, as if they had
dreams to share.

I cannot remember the last rain.
We are taunted every day by
storms traveling elsewhere.

I want to live in that Elsewhere, where
dust becomes moss and ferns
quiver in the breeze ...

and clouds dance on the earth like
angels of old.

Any God that lives outside your
person is most certainly
trying to sell you something.

Another day without rain, all I can write are
laments—the roses are in full
bloom, yet I can hear the grating sound of
shrews gnawing at their roots, seeking what
moisture is to be found.

I write with a shredded hand, blood on the
page—this kitten, Fledermaus, is my
fiercest critic.

Burying a hen without
ceremony—what shall I
plant on her mound?

The lady bear stood on her hind
legs, belly forward, face lost in a
cloud of cherries.
Oblivious to me, I gave her a
thumb-up—I've been doing the
exact same thing for the past
three days.

Life is a chaos system—
those who would present you with a
map or set of instructions are
missing the point altogether.

Creativity is receptivity.
Receptivity is the opposite of thought, prayer,
speech, action—the flow must be reversed;
the womb must first be receptive in order for
conception to take place.
From this Jewel of Receptivity, all becomes
possible—the universe is our toy, our
child ...
and our art!

A brief afternoon shower—not enough, but the
beleaguered chrysanthemum leaves look
encouraged.

Clouds across the horizon like
underwear hanging on a line—
beneath them the naked mountains.

The charming color of old
tea bags—grateful for what
teeth I have left.

In the early evening, a
solitary frog—
calling in the troops!

An unscheduled cloud graced us with
2 1/2 inches. It's not all I need, but it
certainly changes the scenario.
Tonight the fireflies are high-voltage,
the tree frogs make merry music, and the
cats are close at hand. In the morning the
poppies will paint the sky.

As a gardener I'm rather useless.
Weeds annoy me, but I haven't the
patience to manage them.
Hence I plant things that I know will
survive;

and even then, come harvest time, the
fruit is left to rot on the tree or
vine. But oh, I can spend hours in the
woods, pruning and chatting with the
wild things—

we seem to have more sensibilities
shared than I do with the likes of
tomatoes and cabbage.

A mason bee battles a poppy—
and the opium wins.

In a world ruled by monsters, it is
best to keep one's cave
always in sight.

The night air remembers the
afternoon rains.

Once the heart is opened, the
power of the Universe is unleashed,
and fear lives no more.

Simone, keeping watch from atop the
truck—for five million years she has
done just that.

The sound of dripping eaves and a
snuggly kitty or two are the
finest bed companions I have known.

A family of six foxes are living under the
abandoned house up the road;
their cries at night make me feel
safe—
and sometimes a longing to venture out in the
dark of the moon to look for
romance and adventure.

With even the slightest rain, this year's
chrysanthemum and nettle harvest looks
promising.

Upon the horizon, distant
explosions of lightning;
just outside the screen door, the
mini-flashes of lightning bugs—
some nights illumination prevails.

In times such as these, stick close to
nature; in all times stick close to
nature.

All worlds are made by God, but the
world of man has an arrogance about it that
hardens the heart and senses.

Hearing the baby foxes this afternoon, striking out into
the woods with their pre-pubescent
cry—

Thoreau would understand, Whitman would
understand, Basho and Han-Shan would
understand;

hermits and tree-huggers are the
finest among us.
All worlds are made by God,

but it is in the purest arts of man, and the
innocence of nature that His Hand is
most readily felt.

The dark moon
casts an eternal light.

A soft rain falls on our new dawn redwood—
and like a stalk of precious ferns, she
shimmies with delight.

This young redwood tree will live to see the
destruction of civilization, the great mass
extinction, the years of clean-up, the
reintroduction of species, and of their careless
caregivers ...

and I'll be standing beneath her boughs,
shovel in hand, the way I have done so
many many times before.

Black Mountain is ever abuzz with fairs and
festivals,
I show up regularly but rarely feel the
excitement;
no one expects me to have a partner, and
no one expects me to linger long—

back home, in our wood/world, the
kitties and I go about our planting, watering,
weeding, and the subduing of
imaginary dragons.

Life requires so much less than we
believe it does—a hot buttered yam makes a
perfect meal.

Every year, older and uglier—
and yet this inexplicable
contentment!

Bullfrog fussing in the
dark—the very same cadence as a
Christian preacher.

The blue ghost fireflies pour like
fog over the floor of this ancient
bamboo grove,

it's the midnight moon that's
elusive through the canopy of
swaying canes;

ghosts are easy to see in this
world of darkness—

it's the living that pass in and out of
perception.

Religion was invented for crowd
control—no self-respecting
god would belong to one.

This world is a school, nothing
more—we're not graded on our
achievements, but on our
adherence to Truth.

The spring flush of roses has passed, the
opium is in full flower;
in spite of the drought, seedling
Camellia sinensis are popping up like tiny
green mushrooms;

no cicadas yet, but the tree frogs
serenade the crickets.
In the murky dark pond, orange
torpedoes of koi aim threateningly at
islands of hyacinth.

One juvenile bullfrog floats, spun by
currents I cannot see;
in the distance, a fox barks an angry
response to a passing train.
Everything is in its place—

time for my afternoon can of saké.

All day watering the back forty,
exhausted in this enervating sun and
heat;

still, I manage to plant more things that will
need to be watered—and dodge
rainbow brigades of dragonflies carelessly
floating upon even the
vaguest of breezes.

I adore my friends with Asperger's;
I adore obsession.
Certainly, one can blah one's way through
life—as most people do—

but how wonderful to explode with
passion, as a God creating a universe from
nothing more than intention and the
elusive cosmic dust.

There are cats, dogs and people I will
miss until the day I die.
Thank God for death, or these tears of
grief would someday fill an
ocean;
"Tell me about it!" God said—who, after
all, filled the oceans.

Hot, so damned hot the chickens have
quit laying—who can blame them?
Fledermaus comes up from the
woods panting like a dog;
as soon as I water one row, the preceding
row is already dry.

Alas, it is a philosophical quandary that
if you catch a breeze it is no longer a
breeze;
all one can do is to stand with an air of
vulnerability and hope a passing
cloud crawls down your shirt.

We are born with honesty—
and die when we
run out of cunning.

Some nights sleep won't come—
but there are always dreams to
fall back on;

and when those grow dim, there is a
stillness deeper than sleep, where
even shadows appear as light, where the
silence itself is a symphony of
blissful recognition—

where the Rose becomes
intoxicated by its own
scent.

A young bullfrog in the
bedroom—cats
in an uproar.

It comes with a body, pain and grief—
but what we choose to attribute it to is
entirely up to us.

Even in this drought and heat, it is
time to harvest the tea.

In youth I was hard, in age I am
soft—
Lao Tzu would approve.

Heat and drought—
the buds on the
roses are drying shut.

I mistakenly shaved my beard, thinking
someone young and handsome
lived beneath.

Forced inside by the
no-see-ums, I
daubed saké on the welts.

I planted a crabapple tree in the
chicken coop, giving the hens more
shade options—I sure hope it
likes nitrogen!

No temples at the Abbey—
we pray beneath trees.

Every year breaks a new record; the end of the
world is not designed for pleasantries.

I spend all the time I can carrying buckets, schlepping
hoses, and wielding shears to cut away the
carnage.

My pond is a terminal for parched critters; the
koi and newts have become quite the hosts!

Frigid winters, scorching summers, drought and
floods—

The song of the cicada is both defiant and
rapturous.

This year's foxes roam the neighborhood,
yelping with abandon, setting off the

white trash dogs on their chains and ropes in
lonely backyard lots—

freedom is sorely resented by
those who have yet to find it.

I was a love without a lover,
and then a lover without a love;
now I am merged, and the
heavens weep with joy.

Who is lonely now?
—the seed has burst into the
Sky.

The earth strokes my feet, the
stars comb my hair ...

I tell myself stories—wild tales which I
always believe,
and every night sing myself to
sleep.

Who is lonely now?
—the lover and the Beloved are
One.

Three cats torment a
wee mouse
and the crickets keep singing.

Eternity's not so tough—
unlike time, it requires
no management.

It's a truism about mortal
life: you can never
kiss too much

—and you will need all
that expertise upon
reaching heaven!

The inebriation of Truth is almost
more than I can bear—
some of us drink to get sober.

I spent the afternoon on a mountaintop with
two gnomish saints, naming the
trees and rubbing the bellies of three
very smelly dogs—how perfect the laughter of
those who have completed the journey!

I am no longer a poet,
I am *the* Poet.

When one is finally cured, does one
go on taking the medicine?
From the point of Perfection, what
requires fixing?

What is this Light in the darkness?
these worlds within worlds?
colors beyond our drab mortal
spectrum?

Sacred is secret, but holiness
abounds and cannot be defiled;
one mustn't let the flesh of a
thing obscure what is innately, intimately
naked.

Some itches go away when you
scratch them, others just dive
deeper.

I have scratched until there are
holes in the fabric; the
threads have comes loose and the
buttons have hit the floor—

what is left to hold up?
I am no longer a poet,
I am *the* Poet.

Love is the only reality,
whether we choose to acknowledge our
participation or not.

Endless days of oppressive heat and
drought—
can a heart melt?
or does it simply dry up and
blow away?

The man who goes to bed hungry wakes
up knowing he is hungry—the day is
his;

the man who goes to bed glutted wakes up
groggy and stupid—his day has no
joy.

I choose to remain hungry—*What's for
dinner tonight, Lord?
—never mind, surprise me!*

Days in the 90s—the world's
on fire!
O Mother, lead me to Cloud Forest
Hermitage and let me never
depart!

Pulling a tick off my scrotum and
daubing the wound with helichrysum
oil;

much time in the woods today, watering and
adding to my redwood forest—Fledermaus
scampering about like she was born for
this.

I met a box turtle I had rescued from the
road two summers ago—with the remnants of
someone's initials painted on her
shell—

delighted she is faring well by our
pond. In the pond, a brown water snake—
which explains why all the smaller
koi have disappeared;

Spirit eats and breathes and
frolics—but when will She
bring us rain?

Two old pines trees dying and
riddled with beetles and
worm—
I plant a young redwood
between them.

Two barren springs in a row—
only the chestnuts show
signs of growth.

Reading Buson—
distant train—
mosquitoes devouring my toes.

Can one ever have
too many weeping cherries?

Harvesting opium seeds—
nettles are next—
summer comes without rain.

I visit the doctor regularly,
but rarely do what he says—
obstinance keeps me healthy.

Even in the stillness of the
woods I hear the
    thrum of creation—
the cicadas have
    begun to hatch.

In the night breeze through the
screen door, the candle flame
dances—and this black kitten
sucks on my belly.

It has become hard to remember those
young years in which I
thought I would live forever.

Pulling hitchhikers out of
Nina's fur, she
bites me and purrs at the
same time.

The samurai sword by the
back door needs a
proper dusting.

Who's to say what
love looks like?
—sometimes it has claws.

A day of anticipating rain that
never happened—and now a
day behind in my watering ...

Confusion is only brought about by the
rejection or denial of
what is.

Love knows its own, but
sometimes shyness obscures the
courtship.

All of life is a play of clouds in an
eternally blue sky—
hang on to none, for the ephemera of
existence by default knows
nothing but change.

Gladiolas,
the Roman candles of flora,
ever ascending.

Perceiving the nothingness of the
illusion, all concepts become
metaphor;
all concepts being metaphor, what is
life ... but poetry!

A maelstrom of white feathers in the
woods;
some neighbor is missing a
chicken or a duck—while some plump
hawk takes an afternoon nap.

A dozen poems a night, but who will
read them?

—a warm, windy night, three kitties on the
bed, a mug of curry leaf tea with
honey—

who gives a fuck who
reads them?

Sometimes God masquerades as
friends of mine who
say they are atheists who
hate it when I write about
God.

Nina and Shikibu join me on an
afternoon stroll through the
summertime fields, panting like dogs
under every bush and
tree.

This bruised and bitten body finds
solace in a salty hot bath—
but my mind dissolves in a
cloud of steam, which
hovers a while and then is gone.

Archimedes bathes Nina's face until it
shines like obsidian—
he's a good, if reluctant, uncle.

A beautiful black snake today didn't
seem to mind being held and
admired, before
sending her off in search of
shrews.

Today I met a second spring nest of
yellow jackets—
now both ankles are swollen equally.

Bliss is never the end of the
journey, but a happy bowl of
soup along the way.

Not much drought news here—
I watered today what I
watered yesterday.

The advantage to having no plan is that
one then has nothing one has to
stick to.

Personally, I've never been a fan of the
way that God conducts his
universe.

But what's to be done? Once you start
messin' with Perfection, things can get
seriously screwed up.

To speak with absolute clarity, one must
forget all one knows.

To write with absolute certainty, one
must trust one's Pen.

If kitties wielded swords, they
would be entirely too
fierce to manage.

Too tired to sleep, I write
useless poems and
listen to far-off thunder.

A quarter inch of rain did little to
mitigate a half-year drought, although it
did up the humidity on this
vulgar, blaring day:

Where is my mountain hermitage in the
clouds?
from which cumulonimbus do the
immortals, pitying, look down?

Naked in front of the fan I share with
three kitties—from the wide open
window, nothing but darkness.

Hidden behind heart-shaped
leaves, a bumper crop of
mulberries.

Dry spring and now summer—
watering watering watering—I have
neglected to harvest the tea.

Every day my fill of golden
raspberries, while the
chickens watch from their coop.

Today a trek through the Brevard
rainforest—it was
sunny, nary a cloud.

Once Perfection is perceived,
for what and to whom does one
pray?

An open blossom finds its bee,
and the fruit therein does
feed the world.

Once Home is found, all
doors are open, and all
roads lead never away,

but always *To.*

Peace prevails,
albeit not in the storms of dueling
religions, industries, tribes and
nation states; Peace prevails where
one is not looking, seeking or
striving.

Peace prevails,
though rarely perceived in the world of
man and nature; Peace prevails in the
heart of all things, for out of Peace have
all things come.

Although never "attained," and
never the "result of"; when all is
said and done: Peace prevails.

Is there a twelve-step program for
people who are chronically
abused by their cats?

Back to back thunderstorms all
evening, and now the steady drip drip drip off
the eaves;
here in this world of relentless causation we
take pleasure in the sanctities of the
determined—and patiently await the
Kiss of divine intervention.

It is the middle of July and one single
cloud covered the deck in an inch of
hail.

Of course the ice melted before I could
build a snowman or break out the
sled—
it had been 95 degrees an hour
before.

Still, such an event reminds one of the
ephemerality of that which we
confidently refer to as normal.

July melancholy—
this year's mantises are
already half-grown.

Our opera has won another national
award, the highest for a new work;
I have become obsessed with planting
redwood trees—and the creation of a
primordial forest.

If one walks around in circles long
enough one will eventually catch one's
own tail—
what have I to do with this world:
poet, gardener, steward of cats ...?

I am this and I am that; we only
imagine the distinctions.

A massive storm assaults—finally—three
inches in the rain gauge so far; the
  house rattles with thunder—kitties are not
amused.

Wild orange oil in the diffuser, electricity in
the air; *Why write poetry?*—I am
  quite happily inept at most anything
else.

When it is not raining, I dream of rain; when it is
raining, what is there to
  dream of? All that I am I have become—all that
I have become I am.

Tonight the devas are with us, tonight the
mountains shake and the forest and
  gardens dance; tonight the
kitties will snuggle especially close:

Dream? I think not!

  Sunny morning after a night of gentle
rain, sky full of twittering
  swallows; sunflowers in flower, cats in the
most decorous poses upon table, railings and
  post:

today is the opposite of war, and all
  armies rest beneath the tree of
equanimity—
  plotting their next brave adventure.

On such a definitively moist day I cannot
help but move plants around, it's
how I dance with the garden, on this
fecund dance floor we call our
Mother;

it's like nurturing babies, separating and
waltzing trees and shrubs about, knowing
that some day they will be too big to
dance with, and tower above me like a
child come home to bury his
              parent.

Sometimes I would see them a hundred
years hence—other times I could
keep them in a pot forever;
but for now I tuck them in, water them
well, and wish them strength and
              beauty.

War is an illusion—
but then, so is peace.

The time for philosophy is
ended—Joy must
live without restraint.

Brother Tom is off to the mountains in
central China, Brother Ken leaves in the
morning for Colorado, Brother
Aaron has just had his first son born—
what joy I take in my cat-filled bed!

At home in this land of dreams, I
amuse myself with the peccadilloes of the
garden, the kitties, the woods and the
squirrels:
here is always now; now is always
here—shadows only serve to define
that which is illumined.

Always have I gardened, though rarely for
money,
always have I written, though rarely for
recompense;
always have I cared for cats, always have I
danced on windy shores—rarely does
money cross my path, never have I lacked.

Money won't be with us much longer—
song and dance will be with us
always.

Always something to do—*Now what?*—*Now what?*
the future is such a task-master!

Wait all year for these poppies to bloom—hail comes and
strips the petals to the ground—*Now what?*

I plant saplings, imagining their shade in
fifty … one-hundred years;

I go to bed, dreaming of my morning tea ...

With staff or shovel, I visit the
woods daily, often with a cat or
two, sometimes a cocktail;
deer meet me there, and foxes, and on
occasion a bear—in this
land of flailing mortals, nature is a
salve to spirit and song!

All these years, decades, growing old—
and now here I am!

All day picking aronia, blackberries,
blueberries, currants; boiling, mashing, and
straining them into jelly.
I rarely eat jelly, but it's good practice—and
all these fruits deserve a proper ending.

Comfort creates trust in the illusion,
it must be monitored carefully.

Over time there accumulates an amazing
personality—but to
what and to whom does it belong?
The drone of the cicadas is
steady and sure.

Full moon after a rain—the night is a
glowing fog, in which fireflies
float like votives on a roiling sea.

Cicadas thrum the night—
follow their chant to its source and
creation is yours!

Breathtaking love moves my day—
at night, a
buckwheat pillow.

Naked in the orchard—
my hair now as
long as robes.

Beauty is fleeting, but where would we
be without it?

Lao Tzu would say that beauty begets
ugly—but in a world full of
ugly, is beauty not then our salvation?

In moments of revelation, they
both indeed come to the same thing—
for all is imbued with the Divine;

but still I relish a flower in passing,
or a kiss that may
never come again.

Eating too much,
drinking too much—
not thinking about much.

Clever cats
lure me to bed
with the pretense of sleep.

The sweat of the orchard,
the sweat of the stove—
two gallons of aronia jam.

Adolescent bullfrog in the
rain pot that the cats
drink from—not wise.

Mid-July—
there is always room for
one more hydrangea.

Summer evening—
new friends, with little in common
but a penchant for drink.

Smiling for the
photographer—
missing teeth be damned.

The hummingbird moth,
such a dandy poseur—
I wonder if the flowers notice.

So what if I've gotten
fat—of what authority is a
skinny monk?

Crying in the movie because the
young actor has
recently died.

All summer long, year after
year, mowing the
same fucking
grass—
has anything changed?

Do the crickets and the
frogs and the cicadas
listen to one another?

Two black cats on my
bed—were they crows, I would
be Odin!

Sometimes drunk looks like sober,
sometimes sober looks like
insane;
sobriety is never the goal—
inebriation is often the
only way to find one's way
Home.

Life is an itch,
you scratch it till it bleeds—
and still it itches.

Weeds and grasses so thick in the
orchard—cats move like
sharks beneath.

Infinity seems too short a time to
express this magnitude of
Love.

The nature of one's art changes radically
once one realizes that there is
nothing to be angry about.

Nights so hot even the cats won't
snuggle; outside, plants wilt, flowers
bloom and then close right up—
the earth is burning, and
flooding, and turning to dust;
in my heart, the misty mountains stand
foreboding, yet inviting.

It must never be forgot that
Yeshua ben Yosef was a
revolutionary, and that love
has always been the most
radical of all teachings.

In old age, beauty is
more inspirational than
motivating.

Blocking the fan, a
sleeping cat—
guiltless.

Landing on the Rose of
Sharon, a butterfly seems
content to repose.

Brushing what teeth I have
left—outside, the bullfrogs
go on with their courting.

Shortly after dusk a fox began
yeowling—
is he searching for a mate?
or complaining about the
one he has?

A distant train whistle blows—
the cicadas take no notice.

If I come across as flirtatious,
forgive me,
it's just that I find life to be so
very very
sexy.

Sunflowers are exploding—
bumble bees hang immobilized with
exhaustion.

At 61 years, I have
forgotten the stories behind
half these scars.

At 61, even my
tattoos are not all
where they used to be.

Every tree in the orchard has some
blight or another—
still, in springtime they
all come into bloom with the same
wild abandon.

When I die, what then will
mosquitoes eat?

Does the hummingbird seem to
flit more nervously, now that the
gladiolas have ceased blooming?

I am always torn between the desire to
disappear and to appear.
I write poetry as a bridge between the
two—
nothing is ever decided,
one does not exist without the
other.

The world is heating up, seasons are
changing, but not in the agreed-upon
fashion;

how much longer do we have? It is
time to repair to Cloud Forest
Hermitage—

at the very end, who will bury this
impoverished poet? or will he simply
walk away on tree tops?

The rains have come and the
earth is wet—now, a field of
pampas grass to slay!

Faux pas: I clap my
hands in joy,
the cats flee in terror.

There is nothing wrong with a good healthy
addiction, we are made up of
same—it can be said that life itself is an
addiction;

but the severity, the stronghold, certainly
lessens when one has made
peace with said dependence.

When one has come to recognize one's
self as neither this nor that, of what
consequence is an addiction—no matter
how severe?

Embrace all,
but hold on to nothing.

No need for incense on a
night when the
spruce trees are wet!

A lifetime spent herding
cats—what karma could possibly
remain unatoned?

There is always a light at the
end of the world—for those who are
willing to say goodbye.

Joy can only exist within the
presence of spontaneity.

I don't have to write poems, they
write themselves—I am merely my
pen's amanuensis.

The trees this August evening are
dead still, attentive, methinks, to the
droning of cicadas—
and a single note from our
chromatic wind chime.

The grid is down tonight, no
computer, no TV, no telephone, the
only light that of candles and an
oil lamp—oddly, the kitties nap as if
nothing were amiss.

Were there not ghosts, the
living would have no one to
boast to.

From the Qinling Mountains of Central
China, 3 peach seeds, genetic progenitors of
all things peach (more golden than
gold, more precious than jade, rarer than the
feathers of the phoenix); a friend's gift of
immortality—that fits in the
palm of my hand!

There's nothing shameful about
eating well, or taking care of one's
body—unless, of course, it stifles one's
       joy.

Even on a starless night, the
moonflowers light up my
doorway.

Watching my favorite film, crying in
all the same places—
The Last Station.

Were it not for this fat
kitty, would I
know when to go to bed?

When a government jails its
heroes, the way the
church once jailed its saints,
sedition, like heresy, becomes the
noblest of virtues.

Poverty has always been my
friend, it has kept me out of much
trouble—and now leaves me with
few needs; winter brings its
own rewards.

A purring cat—
what more does an evening need?

On this sultry night even the
cicadas sound
tired, diminished.

How annoying, this
young visitor,
disturbing my sleep.

A cat is a sacred object that fits in
any niche, more animated than a
ceramic Buddha or Mary, that
never presumes to
answer your prayers;

there is more sanctity in being
ignored by a feline than in being
ignored by a plastic saint.

And for just a modicum of food and
daily devotions, a house may be
blessed for many a year.

UT FELIS PAX VOBISCUM.

Time is wasted only if spent in
regret or resentment.

Autumn comes early this year, I can
feel it. It is still summer and the
cherries are dropping their leaves—the
maples too;

fires consume California, floods
inundate Louisiana—maybe
winter will be kind this year, and
freeze our ceaseless tears.

Karma flanks the world, no action is
without its consequences;
 good deeds may bring rewards, but
rewards just slow your gait.

Who can sit in the garden and not
notice the roses?
Who can walk a mile and reach no
destination?

We are all bugs here, we eat the
leaf until the leaf is gone—and
 with it, the season: surrender to
Winter and be cold no more.

Day after day I water I weed I mow I
plant—who knew my roots would
 grow so deep?
and still the wind blows me hither and
yon.

Is not love the reason we open our
eyes in the morning?
 and do we not go to sleep with the
hope to meet her in our
 dreams?

Love is not for the faint-of-
heart, but for the
victorious in battle!

Occupying this ruin of a
body reminds me that
time takes no prisoners—
but frees the willing.

My hair grows longer but it
cannot grow any whiter;
how many snows left before the
end of the world?

Gravity is just something that
keeps us down, we must
learn to take it more lightly;
flight requires neither faith nor
trust—it is simply what
occurs when one ceases to
        fear the Sky.

Making love with yourself is
never a bad thing;
just remember to kiss a lot, in all the
right places—and don't be in
such a hurry to leave afterwards.

There's no need to look at the
thermometer to tell whether you are
cold or hot;
where you now sit, you are neither
north nor south, east nor
west.

Must you look at the ingredients to
tell whether your lunch is too
sweet or too salty?
why then do you ask God whether
you are right or wrong?

I hate to squash a mosquito in its
moment of bliss and harmony,
but then I remember that my hand is a
divine whip, which God moves
without judgement or restraint;

SLAP!—and another wee soul
graduates to a more agreeable
form.

If there's one thing we should never
judge, it's another being's
capacity for love;

we know as much about a cat's soul or a
cow's soul or an owl's soul as we
know about our own.

All that we can ever really know about
another being is the love that they
awaken in our own heart:

to awaken is to love;
to love is to awaken.

There is nothing quieter than
resting in God's arms—it is the
deepest of silences, and the
absolutest of
joys.

One who has viewed Eternity becomes
fearless, invincible,
and happy to put another quarter in the
jukebox, and dance until the whole
café is on its feet.

God is not like water, which wets you and
then dries in the sun; rather, more like
fire, which burns you further every time you
get close, with an end game that only
ashes will understand.

Unlocking the doors to Eternity requires
neither scheme nor aggression,
but merely a laying down of arms.

Nothing grays one's hair like
lamenting your youth.

Live in poverty, and worry how to eat;
make money, worry how to
spend it—poverty and wealth aren't the
issue, worry is!

I get my wisdom from the trees: when it
rains, I grow; when in drought, dig
deeper! When winter comes, do not
resist.

Seasons change of their own, life takes
care of itself; nothing lasts for
long—but the seed of Truth is
planted day after day after day.

Alcohol makes me undizzy,
coffee puts me to sleep,
 eating makes me hungry;
I have learned to not put much stock in
what people say about the world.

Atheists are too religious for my
comfort, religious people too
damn mean—only God requires
nothing of me and allows my
 heart to sing.

The fireflies are gone—
I am certain that the
 stars miss them.

1. Three handsome young bartenders vying for my
attention—
why can't we just take turns?

2. Three handsome young bartenders vying for my
attention—
I fear I may get embarrassingly drunk.

3. Three handsome young bartenders vying for my
attention—
but which one is to drive me home?

This year's gardens are quite
ahead of me—
only winter can fix this!

It is stunning, this symphony of
life—may my every
breath be my applause!

In this world of loss, what is
there to do but
accept what is given?

One does not come to wisdom by
clinging to a religion or a
code; we sit in nature—does
nature have morality?
Nature is simply present with
itself—as we should
be.

Love itself is absolute,
and thus requires neither
tokens nor promises.

August rains have hatched an
infestation of fleas; the cats
scratch me, I scratch the
cats—everybody's itching.

We are all parasites on this good
planet; another hurricane
batters the coast—*scratch scratch
scratch*;

where does it end, this
taste for blood?

Partial acceptance of Truth is
meaningless;
acceptance of partial Truth is
nonsense—
once the Truth is perceived, all
else falls away; once the
Truth is received, the
game is over.

From addiction to addiction we
wander, yanked about in
ten thousand directions;
one glimpse of Suchness changes
everything—see how the sky
clears after a storm!

Paradise writes its name over
yours—to get lost there is the
privilege of the single-minded.

The largest tree on our property came down in
last night's wind; the trunks are too thick to
cut through, but I spent the afternoon limbing the
beast in an attempt to save what can be
salvaged of the trees and shrubs that got
crushed and pinned.

Nature has a way of shaping my day, a
cocktail and epsom salts bath my
evening;
why ponder the universe when the universe comes
to you? Sorrow and joy chase each other's
tails—and love pervades the ethers.

Five cats on the
bed—
it must be autumn.

The pumpkin vine by the
chicken coop
is starting to scare me.

Few of my plans have ever
panned out—which has been good
incentive to stop making them.

Few of my loves have ever stayed
true—which has taught me to
look for something deeper than
"love."

Sometimes easy, sometimes
difficult; sometimes blissful,
sometimes angst-ridden—

I have learned neither to
run toward nor from; and by
not resisting, to return always to
this Immaculate Center.

Do joy and
sorrow
ever unlock hands?

Has this world ever
not been run by
liars, murderers and thieves?

Any religion that does not espouse love for
all sentient beings is not only bogus, but
treachery to the soul.

The sun falls on all in its path;
the rain and wind feed all life
equally.

The True Poet writes for devil and
angel alike; for in this grand book,
all have a page.

In this forest of
nothingness,
why look for trees?

Of love, knowledge, and power, love is the
greatest, for it is the surest gateway to the
other two.

In this world of toil and chaos, one's
center of gravity must be
remembered always as that which
neither moves nor
wants.

True passion comes from an
awakened heart,
nothing else.

Look at my heart, it remains ever
still, the audience for which
all of creation dances.

White pine tree,
200 feet tall,
with a moon at the very top!

An entire spring and summer without
rain. Trails have turned to dust, moss
gone brown. Summer's not ended and
trees are shirking their withered
leaves.

Who can bear this lifeless world?
Join me, if you will, at
Cloud Forest Hermitage.

It is easy to be bored with predictable
humanity;
nature alone continues to
surprise me—
and cats, always cats.

Sleeping cats in the brisk evening
breeze, exhausted from an afternoon of
watering and the slaying of pampas in the
back forty ... no, wait ... that was
me ... the cats merely

supervised, and made the occasional
troll patrol. Either way, supervising can be
exhausting—which is why I like my
hands in the dirt, feeling the pulse of the
earth unrattle my senses;

life and death in nature go hand-in-
hand—these sequoias may live for a
thousand years; this worn-out body may be
ashes at their feet tomorrow—what is
there to worry? The seasons

manage what is theirs to manage.

Alcohol they say dulls the senses,
but sometimes the senses need a
dose of dulling;
other intoxicants distort the senses, but
sometimes a bit of distortion looks
more like "reality."

What is sobriety? it is often the
farthest thing from the truth.
And when the Truth is laid bare, neither
intoxication nor sobriety will
save you!

Whenever you have the
opportunity, get drunk with a
saint.

For God's sake,
stop being
who you were.

I have little interest in things which must be
proven—but much for that which is
beyond refutation.

61 years isn't old, *per se*, but I've been
rough with myself;
friends say I wear it well, but I
feel it in my joints and myriad
scars.

Summers grow hotter and winters
colder; I may choose not to
adopt any more pets unless they are
agèd.
As for lovers, they have been legion—

it is time to let the trees
sing me to sleep.

God acted surprised when I told Him I
knew where he was hiding.
Oh, not to worry, we've been playing this
game for a very long time—
in truth, He likes to let me win;

but enjoys me all befuddled—
laughs, then sticks out a
foot and trips me when He
catches me being
rational.

Is that an owl outside or
Archimedes,
snoring upon my bed?

Hacking grasses all day, bare legs in
briars, watering my dying
orchards and harvesting wild
grapes for jelly;
when I finally come to bed the cats
chastise me for being late—
tomorrow will look much the same.

God spare us the religiosity of
atheists—and the godlessness
of the religious!

Bugs devour me by day, at night I
dream of missing friends;
bliss comes not from this world, but from
something ancient and unseen.

Still, there's toast and jam in the
morning, and tea with honey and
cream.

And any conversation that delves
beyond the words reminds the
heart that it was made for
dancing.

The winter wood has arrived, but still no
rain; the mowing is done, but the
chrysanthemums have yet to bloom.

Everywhere are hurricanes and
floods, drought and fire;
here we just wait—expecting nothing.

Tomorrow, they predict, the market will
crash.

I've never been much for associating labor with
recompense—we do what we do, what we
enjoy, and the universe provides;

it is kindness, not gold, that is our
worthiest investment.

One doesn't have to believe in life to
live, nor in love to
embrace the Moon.

The old monk's in the hospital, still no
rain, the world's at war, its
people unhinged;

three glasses of gin and a Jane
Austen novel later, I parlay with the
cats on my bed, the

door open to a cool night
breeze—the cicadas have yet to
abandon their song.

The world is divided on this: some say that
being a poet is a noble and even glamorous
profession,

other, perhaps wiser sages say it is a
loathsome and ridiculous enterprise that
impoverishes both body and soul;

I myself feel that neither nobility nor
poverty are relevant, for life itself is merely
metaphor—which leaves the

poet one-up on existence, and neither
humble nor proud to embody the
profundity of God's verse.

Joy never comes from planning, but rather at the
point in which all plans have been
abandoned.

Cat beings safe on the bed, coyote beings
calling from the mountain across the
valley, a night in which

all tasks are done. Happiness, sadness, for the
moment they do not enter here—heaven,
hell? neither commits my soul.

People going left, people going
right, people being born, people dying;
people climbing the stairs, people descending the
ladder:

Who can make sense of all this coming and
going?
Beneath this gingko tree on a bed of
soft yellow leaves, eternity

passes on the back of a woolly worm.

My Guru told me I was already
there, and so I have stopped
coming and going;

maps are curious things, now that
all roads lead
home.

Hurricane Matthew batters the coast:
even here in the distant mountains leaves are
ripped from the trees;

and yet in the eye of the storm, they say, all is
quiet and still. Who will stand here with
me until our very

souls have been stripped bare?

Here at Graybeard Abbey I lose track of the
times and styles; pop music sounds like
noise now, and when I read I stick to the

classics. Neither famous nor particularly
talented, I stack up this year's
squashes for inspection.

Neither in love nor desirous to be, I
sleep with an overweight kitty purring by my
pillow. I don't ask for much: if I can

feed my cats I am happy; I have few
friends and even fewer enemies; the more I
drink, the more sober I get;

when the economy crashes I will harvest
acorns, should the sky fall I will
collect the stars in a basket. I have

sorrow and I have joy, and that is
      enough.

This world is run by petulant children, who neither
understand Truth, nor bow to
Mystery—

what kind of paradise is
fashioned by greedy fingers?

—my country is Cloud Forest Hermitage, though there is
neither flag nor boundary; but don't
look for me there—the wise will see naught but

clouds, trees, mountains ...

Today I met my favorite actor—
God, masquerading as
myself.

Anyone who believes there is an
answer hasn't fully
understood the question.

Grief is a well with no
bottom, neither water to
quench one's thirst.

Chilly night, two sick kitties;
autumn is thrust upon us—
if not for cats, I would have chosen a
healthier planet.

At 61, I am older than I thought I would
ever become; my list of mistakes and
embarrassments is vast, epic.
In my time I have tried all, done all, and
followed every dream and fantasy.

Now, I find, it is the simple undoing of
things that brings me the greatest
pleasure, and the time in which nothing
remains to be done that I find most
useful and most assuredly pleasing.

Only God is; all of creation exists in a
state of perpetual grace.

Sometimes I drink too much; sometimes I
go to bed with dirty feet;

all things bow to That, all action
bespeaks That.

To remember Self is to learn how to
live—

all else is mere vanity.

Dancing around a
brush fire—
these pagan cats and I.

To be governed by dishonest persons naturally brings
distrust;
return to nature and Truth is revealed.

Trees, mountains, animals, clouds ... none know
deceit; a person who cannot sit quietly on a stump has
no clarity to give.

There is nothing of any significance that cannot be
learned from observing a
tadpole;

Only in times of honesty can Peace prevail.

I've lived a hundred wondrous places, but have
never found Shangri-La—
perhaps I am yet not ready to relinquish suffering.

In the black pond waters, a
single koi, uncertain which
way to turn.

As a souvenir of summer, a
lingering hornet takes a
piece of my foot.

At summer's end, the melodious
cicadas have given way to the
cricket's tedious drone.

An evening catterel *:

Of 7 cats and kittens, not one does
as she's told;
I wonder what an 8th would do if
given half a scold.

[* a feline *doggerel*]

Entirely unmannered,
this year's bear shits right in the
middle of the path.

Like paper rain,
the plummeting
poplar leaves.

Sylvan mystery, the holly
grove—one can piss or poop or
jack off with impunity.

Above the rock with the Cherokee
petroglyphs, a
surprise cache of passionfruit!

Tired of my reading, Archimedes
falls asleep with his
face on my book.

The tea orchard is in full, effulgent bloom—
and aren't the bees thrilled and surprised to
have such aureate fodder this time of year!

Simultaneously, the plants are dropping seeds from
last year's flower-fest—which I am
prepping for sprouting over winter.

What more could one ask from a tree that
gives year-round—that wakes you each
morning and sets you on the path?

Cats! these nocturnal beasties:
by day they sleep—
at night, I have no idea what books they read!

There are so many things I could be
doing—but sitting in the woods seems
infinitely more pressing.

Sometimes love is hidden by the shadow of a
thought—but it is always there when the
shadow fades.

As my body softens with age, so does my
heart, for with each lover's death, some
candle was lit—which all now
            burn in perpetuity.

Why speculate on life when death is
so near? —why speculate on death when
life is so dear!

Dark, the autumn,
with no fireflies.

Sometimes fighting windmills
is the most
logical thing to do.

Exquisite Love is not found where
one is looking, but rather
blooms from the inside out;

just because one cannot see God's
face, does not mean He has not
shown it to you:

always Love is there, beckoning.

The simple poet writes simple poems to
underscore the simplicity which
underlines that complexity which
doesn't really exist;

all praise to the little things that
remind us of that vast Joy that
exists without cause or effect:

May all beings know happiness, the
simplicity of joy, and the joy of
          simplicity!

It is the trust of an animal that
makes me feel most
successful as a human.

Is being authentic not the ultimate virtue?
—the universe itself revolves around the
font of authenticity.

The first frost just barely
averted, the pumpkins
glisten with morning dew.

Alas, summer is a lost cause—
but I will hang on to autumn as
long as I am able.

When cats do our bidding, only
then will we know we have
evolved into masters.

Real love reminds us that
we have never been
incomplete.

Forgetting the hand, the writer
becomes the pen; forgetting the
pen, the writer becomes the ink;

forgetting the ink, the writer
becomes the words; forgetting
the words, the writer becomes

a poet.

The True Poet abides in nature—the
world of man is far too prosaic,
though he may occasionally venture to
converse with lovers—but even
then the intellect all too often
holds dominion—or on the rare
occasion an artist, poet, dancer,
composer ... but only if that one is
irretrievably mad.

Today's harvest: green tea, nettles, lemon
verbena, tulsi, and copious chrysanthemum
blossoms, layer upon layer in the
dehydrators, my array of teas for the
upcoming year;

toast and jam before bed, two kitties to
tuck me in, moonflowers outside the
window illuminating our bed—who
would not want to be me on this
lovely, lonely autumn night?

Learning is fun but begets presumption;
my smart friends tend to believe
they are right.
But if none are right, then no one is
wrong;

between questions and answers, questions
are the more promising.
What joy is there in constant
noise, when the silence is so beautifully,
unquestionably complete?

I know, I know! my buddy Lee always
calls me *Gav-Tzu* when I
get like this—
but sometimes it all just seems so
thoroughly and utterly

simple.

Halloween:

Cats at play in autumn leaves, a nearby
doe nosing for forage; how stark the
naked poplars, how blinding the
autumn sun!

A season of drama and flourish,
precursor to winter's endless
stasis and torpor;
we remember the dead, but do the
dead remember us?

Still the rains evade us;
dry as a prison fuck, the
autumn leaves simply
drop without ceremony.

I have died by fire, I have
died by water;
but now I fear we shall
merely turn to dust—

and blow away.

At the shelter, Simone's name was
simply "Pretty Face;" she fit in the
palm of my hand.

Still every bit as pretty, she now
sprawls across my bed like a
mama bobcat.

And like so many who have
shared my bed, she is all too
happy and prone to draw

blood when the mood strikes.
Love is dangerous, but is it
not the pain and the blood that

remind us that we are
alive—and when it is gone, do we not
cherish the very

scars left behind?

It is too late to write poetry;
everything has been stated.
The distant freeway thrums without
pause; the occasional train
rumbles through Black Mountain with its
abrasive, heron-like shrieks.

What have I to say to this ailing
world that hasn't already been
writ? We come and we go like
bees from a hive—
and the hand of Immortality
graciously waves us on.

So much to be seen in this
old cat's loving eyes—
I can hear my heart purring.

'Tis the dark of the moon—
shadows and matter are one in
darkness;
war is rumored—helicopters and
bombers fly overhead daily—
and me, still harvesting autumn
chrysanthemums.

If war breaks out, these poems may
never be read—but the winter wind will
always know their meaning.

One is blessed indeed to live in a
time and place without war;
beside me, a snoring kitty makes the most of it.

The science of making love is less of a
science than a superstition—
best not to think about it.

I have known the wealthiest and the
brightest, and still I prefer the
company of cats;

I have known the talented and most
famous, but a hummingbird on the
hollyhocks makes me clap with joy—

and the chirruping of a solitary
cricket leaves me
breathless.

All bones and withered
flesh are the
woods in winter.

Five cats in bed,
winter has arrived.

The woods in winter: crisp, but not
cold; barren, but not empty;
sleeping, not dead; latent,
unmanifest—
more patient than I.

The drought rages on, one of the
worst in decades—ominous portent of
tribulations to come;

still, our little creek trickles, the
spring-fed pond has not diminished and yet
abounds with newts and

tadpoles. Two murderous monkeys compete for
dominance—but deep in these woods their
shrieks are not heard.

A ten-pound "head" of maitake, gift from the
woods; I've been slicing and dicing all
evening. Three trays in the

dehydrator, two bins in the
fridge—there'll be scrambles and
bisques all week!

In the orchard, a hundred pumpkins await the
first frost; let the planets fall and the
stars collide—here we live with simple

extravagance.

The forecast is dire, still no rain in
sight; leaves are mostly down, the
earth and air both brittle and crisp.

Angels I have petitioned have been
unyielding, their hearts and urns both
barren and dry;

tomorrow I will go have a chat with the
salamanders along the creek, for if
anyone knows something about water,

it would be they.

Tonight, even the crickets are
quiet, afraid to let winter
know where they are hiding.

The mantises are gone, as are the
ladybugs; only the woolly bears
remain—their tiny fur coats.

Though both have their appeal,
I choose simplicity over complexity.

Why do I resent brushing the
few teeth I have left?

Beware the kitty with the
swift right hook, she draws
blood every time.

On the chrysanthemums,
a lone monarch,
seemingly inebriated.

Little hands have
dug up the tea seeds I
planted last week.

An editing job completed, I watch the
movie *Genius* three times in a
row. Tomorrow, elections and civil
unrest; tonight, not a peep from
cricket or frog;
one sleepy cat to comfort me—who
knows how this book will end?

Harvesting pumpkins and raking
leaves, cleaning gutters and pruning
grape arbors; the sky is a filthy brown
cloud—mostly smoke from vast and
myriad forest fires;

not ideal weather for a hot-blooded
Sagittarian, nor what was anticipated when I
returned to Appalachia.

Cocktails and kitties soothe my
nerves; Armageddon looms on every
horizon—but here at
Graybeard Abbey, the roses are still
abloom.

Praying to Universal Mind,
rubbing a fat kitty's tummy—
which is apt to bring me luck?

We all believe what we
want to believe—that's
the nature of belief;

belief is neither fact nor
fiction—it is merely
make-believe.

A clear and present enemy is
preferable to a
latent, sleeping foe.

How I love to sit by a fire or
creek without book or task, thought or
prayer—
if only this pen would
relinquish my hand!

The sight of geese flying in
formation—why do I always
feel like the one left behind?

Chrysanthemum tea, a fire, a
leather couch with a cat at each
shoulder—
when I die, I plan to take my
heaven with me.

In a sea of maple-leaf
confetti, a cat stalks an
invisible foe.

A cold wind pulls through
leafless poplars, the sky as
white as an old poet's
hair;

a black cat perched on a
locust post—an angry
cloud on an autumn
afternoon.

The stomach is an endless
pit, trying to fill it is
futile—
better to simply make friends
with the hollow.

America is poised for a rebirth,
the old religions and the old ways are
no longer fitting—we're going back to
something older than old, something
eternal, from back when God was
just a wild and crazy teenager;

so, please, if you're not ready to
join in the fun, at least stand out of the
way, grab a drink at the bar or
something, just get off the damn
dance floor and let the chariots
arrive—the Kingdom of Heaven is
about to begin.

Fires rage through the mountains, scenic vistas are
now walls of smoke and ash,
the opaque air stings both lungs and
spirit:
dragons have overrun the castle—and neither
rain nor savior to soothe the
burn.

All I ask is for destiny to meet me
half-way;
it's not that I believe in free will or
anything—sometimes I just prefer *my*
version of the tale.

Virtue and vice, now there's an
ugly couple! I'm never certain which I
care for the least,
hence my love of nature, where
neither are welcome.

Two black kitties use each other as
mutual pillows; in the front of the
house the old monk coughs—
what is left to the night but to
blow out the candle and love the dark?

The air the color of dried blood, a few
diaphanous clouds linger, feckless,
above.

Silent, birdless, a kitty stalking through
dried leaves raises a disquieting
racket.

This heartbroken autumn limps into
winter—one lone camellia, in full
bloom!

Fairies in the garden?
or simply the floating seeds of the
milkweed?
—oh no! a cat just
killed one!

Once the last cat is in and fed the
night becomes a sanctuary from the
vicissitudes of the day;
through a bower of trumpet vine the
gibbous orb winks assuringly.

But for the uncertainly of dream we
would be free of this flailing
world; between light and shadow we
find a pillow of stillness to
cradle our earthen head.

This moon, roseate through a smoky
shroud, stars dim and choked; seven
thousand acres on fire—I cannot
remember the last rain—yet in the
quiet of the pond this afternoon, amid a
mosaic of flaming leaves, three wood
ducks spoke of their floating kingdom,
as if the precious water had been made
just for them.

I hate to be rude to spiders,
but they've colonized all my
winter shoes.

Tonight winter arrives with a fury; frigid
gales attack the Abbey from all
directions; what leaves there
were today will be gone
tomorrow, chased off into the gulch.

What warmth there has been is but a
memory now—another spring's joys
pull us forward.

So drunk I can't see straight, all of a
sudden everything becomes perfectly
clear: that which is invariably
feared the most is the absence of an
adversary.

God and his minions never cease to
amuse us with evil and
tribulation, for without such we would
come to no understanding of
good—and peace.

I wonder which category cats fall under?

Feasting on the Formless,
the more one indulges, the
emptier one becomes—
Ah, but the flavors!
Que puis-je dire?

She asked why I write poetry—
Do I?
—who says that the poems don't write *me?*

A gale wind blew away the fallen
leaves;
now the oaks and maples, motionless in their
shame, hum a gentle dirge of
beauty's demise.

Striations of clouds tonight toy with the
Moon, like silken fans concealing a geisha;
what has Heaven to say to the
ruins of the day? Coy as ever, the Moon
grins and moves on her way.

Goblins, orcs, and trolls afoot, but here in our
hovel, on these wee acres, a wood stove
blazing, shadows are friends, and enemies but
empty jars;
tea and vegetables suffice, cats create the
rhythm, and the ode of the Moon makes of
loneliness a hallowed and precious thing.

Only a true heretic can come to God—
at some point religion must be abandoned for
inexpressible Joy!

Crunching through the collage of
autumn leaves, a red-eyed turtle, out for an
adventure on a sunny Thanksgiving
Day;
how enviable the slow and the wise—
for the turtle knows, wherever he
goes, he is always Home.

In the purity of night, a spirit unfettered can
soar to infinite heights;
no star is too far, no time too long and
no love too brief;

dreams are but stories the soul tells itself,
desires and satisfactions to enliven, enlighten, and
amuse—
and pass the time until
waking.

Compassion for oneself is the
beginning of all ends,
patience with oneself mollifies the
monsters,
simplicity is the cure of cures;

a tree blooms in the forest and its
fragrance permeates the
ether, and that which has been
dark becomes illumined with the
nectar of life:

O Mystery, where questions and
answers end!

The holy and the
unholy held a party
and no one came.

for Zane

There's nothing wrong with having
opinions, as long as they are
correct—but this old puss holds
everyone in disdain, and I've never been
tom enough to contradict her.

Beyond distinctions of good and evil is a gibbous
Moon, floating, mid-sky, effulgent, unabashed,
unassailable.

Although I visit these woods daily,
I long ago lost the path.

On the occasion of my 62nd birthday:

Old enough, missing half his teeth, creaky
back and joints, this old monk makes
bed with a circle of cats and listens to the
dripping eaves.

Morning, spring, wealth, fame—what are
these, when the night lies
naked beside me?

Being old and ugly doesn't diminish one's
appreciation for the young and comely—
but it has the advantage of making them
    unattainable.

I feel safe when it rains, nothing can
get me when it rains; thunder rumbles the
house, but lightning never strikes;
creeks flood, rivers rise, but we
live on a ridge.

Guests don't come knocking when it
rains, Jehovah's Witnesses lay low; burglars
don't rob houses, the *federales* don't
storm anyone's doors when the weather is
inclement.

When it rains, I know where all the
cats are—inside; when it rains, soup
froths on the stovetop. When it rains my
gardens gurgle, the devas sing, the
eaves harmonize, and the trees scratch

heaven's belly. In Valhalla, in Hy-brasil and
Shangri-la it must rain every day; in
heaven we abide safe, for there are always
clouds; angels' feathers repel and
protect.

It's not that I resent the sun, I just don't
like it always prying into my
business;
my hair curls when it
rains.

Slashing briars and planting redwood
saplings, the cats frisk and crows
cut up the sky; I grin and look
forward to another night of promised
rain—because sometimes a promise is
          enough.

There are always two dragons, one black, one
white, that chase each other endlessly round and
round, and have done so since before the
beginning of time. One is emptiness, one is
fullness, one is knowing and one unknowing.

To ride one and not the other is to live in
fear; to ride both requires neither harness nor
faith—one merely finds that place where the
earth meets the sky, where the horizon
goes on forever:

there is a wee table there, where fragrant tea is
always served.

Whatever God gave me last night seems to have
worked—I woke up singing, dancing, and ...
more than a little pregnant!

I long ago stopped waiting for God to
call my name; long ago I stopped
calling His.

Now sometimes we wrestle at night;
sometimes we make love, others we simply
fall asleep singing or giggling.

Why dress up a mannequin when the
Naked Truth is breathing in your
ear?

Why flirt with ephemera when one dwells in a
world full of Lips?

Born feral, it has taken me a
lifetime to be domesticated by my
cats.

That I have been unkind in my life makes me
weep,
  that I have suffered makes me glad;
happiness and sadness are just drifting clouds in an
  ever-changing sky:
that I have found Joy makes me something more than
  human at last.

To trust a thing
is to know it is
in you
and you in it
for all time.

The rain on my lashes is like
tears from somebody else's
laughter—
and now me,
dancing like a damn fool!

I have long learned to
sequester my joy—
but, really, what's the point?

What can possibly be more fun than
being God realizing
Himself?

Walking the woods in a light
drizzle, if only to
exercise the kitties;
the unmistakable smell of
bear piss—
freeze-dried berries the colors of a
winter sunset.

What good is a poem if it
does not make you a little less
afraid of the dark?

Surrounding the Abbey, dripping eaves make
musical notes—and here I am,
mumbling lyrics.

The woods in winter:

Dragons leave scars on the trees and
disarray among the lilies in the
pond; unicorns, ever evasive, are
caught only in the perimeter of the
eye, their delicate hoofprints swiftly
swallowed up by damp leaves and
sand.

Elves and faes have retired to their deepest
dens; even Nessie sleeps dreamless in the
black and cold water. The cats, with their
heightened sense of fancy, stalk
creatures unseen.

Stumbling up the trail to build the
evening's fire, I reach down and
pluck, from decaying flora and prickly
vines, a treasure of no small
magnitude:

a lone phoenix feather, portent of the
demise of summer.

Coup d'etat:

Life is after all just a poem, a metaphor.
Do not think that life is the answer—it is
not. Do not think that life will
save you—it will not.
Lifetime after lifetime we persist—we are
merely sharpening the blade.

Don't look to your intellect for an
answer—it has none.
Don't look to books, and certainly not to
your youth, your beauty, your health or
your wealth—they are your deficits!

Lifetime after lifetime we play our
cards, jealously guarding our hand—while the
Joker waits patiently. But winning is not
winning—nor losing losing; such
tropes come to naught.

The barren tree bears no fruit; look rather to the
wind which has stolen her leaves and
fouled her seed.
It is the winter wind which warms the
hearth of Home.

It is surrender, not victory, which
wins the war.

My given name has two meanings, "Prince of
Peace," and "Battle-hawk."
I have spent a lifetime reconciling the two.

from Dobra Tea House of a
December morning, enjoying a dark
Yunnan pu-erh—server, Nancy:

Resist not that which is given
freely—that which has been yours since
before time was time.

I have wandered the streets looking for lovers, and have
found them in the darkest of places;
in the most famous cities of the world, I have met
men, been outraged at their beauty, and humbled by their
acquiescence.

Now, in old age, I find my love in the trees of the
forest, in branches aloft and in roots moist and
fecund with life and breath.
Beauty abounds where hearts are open; Nature always
succumbs to a "Yes."

The Abbey glows upon a drizzly
night, with Christmas lights and
fires stoked—in the gardens, a trillion
moons on every leaf and
blade.

In time, desire becomes surrender, and
all that has been longed for is
received.
Desire heartily, then let your
passion become your peace.

I know it, but can't say it; I write it, but
can't know it—
it moves me, but I remain
unmoved; the seasons change, but the
blossom remains.
In the bottom of a cup of chai, the
universe swirls into existence—
in a single draught, it is
gone.

Noble hawk that screams above my
head, don't listen to the angry crows that
rail against you.
The sky is yours, you have no peer;
even the Sun submits to your
glory.

I myself have no need of flight—
seeing you aloft is quite enough; the Earth
suits me, and I find Sun in the very
soil I till and kiss.

Still, in our way, we share the same
sky—and perhaps the
same cry.

The Moon, isolate, frozen midstream of a
December sky—it's only the
world that keeps turning.

Separating the created from the
creator is taking the dream from the
dreamer—
does one exist without the
other?

Passion, emotion, sentiment ...
these are currents in the
Water—
but still ...
the Water ...

The ridiculously diminutive labels on
bottles my agèd eyes can no longer
read—
but I have become less concerned with
ingredients and distinctions.

Spirituality, sensuality—
neither should be avoided;
neither the destination.

In this vast body called Home, there is no
room for strangers, but all are welcome—
come, enjoy the gardens, the fauna, the
rhapsody of the ages.

Nakedness is what we wear and
innocence who we are;
the world is but a pillow, upon which we
make delicious love.

Love is the epicenter of the
universe, and worlds will
continue to quake until they
have evanesced into
That.

Outside, the Moon:
inside,
the Moon.

Rooted in emptiness, my cup keeps
filling, and I drink!
I drink!

From the vantage of the Sun, there are
no shadows, only bright light,
in every direction.

The time of tribulation has come,
what is there to do but dance like a
dervish upon mountains that
tremble; what is there to do but
embrace the Love which is our
                undoing?

The Lover I sleep with now brings a
nakedness to the bed heretofore unknown to
all my wandering days; He has
restored shine to my faded soul and
made a lifetime of passions appear as
boredom.

What is His name?

Friend, if I knew, I would
surely tell you.

That which we refer to as God cannot be
understood:
smart people thusly question God;
wise people thusly question
understanding.

Approaching the Point of Revelation, all one's
reflections of self become nullified—and yet are
soon handed back, illumined and blessed,
for they too are the treasures of the Creative
Intelligence, and as such, sacred.

Who would know if God touched me?
I wouldn't tell a soul; I don't imagine it would
show on their CT scans or in X-rays.

Who would know if the Secret of
Secrets was in my heart or brain? Would my
eyes disclose, or my drooling mouth?

It's a secret, God said, *keep it hidden;* but
who would know if my world split in two and
only a shadow remained? or if

Love swelled in my gut, like a massive
pimple ready to burst?
Paranoid, I run to the mirror and comb what is

left of my hair,
lest anyone suspect.

Sitting on the front porch of my
Eye, gazing out toward
Eternity, one might wonder when
Eternity is to begin—only to miss the
simplest truth that
Eternity begins
thus.

Terrifying, this Earth, if one
believes oneself to be something
other than a dream of her
        awakening.

Reading books is no substitute for
living in alternate realities.

On a sunny winter's afternoon, walking in the
back forty with Nina, Izumi, and
Archimedes; crows in the giant oak lob
caustic curses and threats;
scats on the path speak of evening
festivities—raccoons, opossums, skunks, fox,
bear ...

we are all travelers here, trying to keep
warm and ahead of the game—what
peace is to be found seeps up through the
earth from roots deeper than all the
tribes and creeds that have ever been or are
yet to be.

Asheville, "Land of the Sky"—
the Moon stops here frequently to
pacify admirers.

All afternoon chopping briars in the
woods—the same briars I chopped last
year;
where do clouds go when they simply
vanish?

Nina, the tiniest kitty, chases the larger
kitties up trees;
Archimedes fusses the entire time—
nature makes his paws
dirty!

Solitude, loneliness, cats in their
finest element;
this has been our Christmas of
choice—time is short, why waste it amid
noise and confusion?

For dinner, a glass of champagne and a
bowl of sticky rice—
there is nowhere to go but here.

If I have had any lifetime not discipled to the
care of kitties and gardens, it is certainly
not worth recalling.

Thieves have infested the temple—or did they
simply never leave?
Here on the farm we trade tea and eggs for
meat and milk;

if someone invades my borders, I make them
coffee—if they make demands, toast and
jam.

It is the people who have the most money that
create the most problems;
when a tree falls, we chop it for wood.

My doors have no locks—no one has ever
come to steal my poverty;
may I die tending my chrysanthemums and
camellias!

Frigid tonight: I gaze out the frosted
window into the dark—
the flame in the distant greenhouse warms my
soul; the greenhouse frogs must be
crooning like drunkards!

Genius is merely a willingness to
live in a house with unlocked doors and
open windows.

Following a heron down into the
woods, I have a hunch why the koi are
decreasing in number;

winter leaves are down, trees in
repose—who ever knows whether there
will be a spring?

In my mind I am always numbering my
cats—anyone unaccounted for and I
pace the farm like a madwoman paces the
beach, awaiting her husband's long lost
ship to return to port.

A Chinese sage once said: Never refuse
wine unless you are already
drunk.

Drunk all the time now, I stand wide-
eyed and sober, shovel-in-hand, happily
moving shrubs and trees about—
yet ever aware of the graves I have
had to dig,

and will surely dig again.

Come New Year's I'd committed to
reading prose again, reading and rereading
the classics; but I've already started

with Isherwood, a friend and mentor for
almost 20 years and one of the finest
prosists in the English language—it's a
shame to have not read his entire
canon—

then on to Joyce, Wolfe and Tolstoy,
men I would have loved to have

known.

But in reading an intro about Chris by
Gore Vidal, another departed friend, I find
myself weeping and have to put the
book down—we live in a realm of
loss and sorrow.

Out on the lawn roses still have
buds, perfect summer buds frozen in
form;

it may be too late to bloom again, but the
blossoms of spring haunt in perpetuity and are
always there for the recalling.

So it has been for ten trillion years,
since the first bud opened—like a book—
and the story of creation began to

unfurl.

Enough wine and even bad wine becomes
delectable—discrimination is a
relative concept;
so it is with life, as so many become
drunk on their own paltry
existence.

Ah! but those who taste that *other*
wine vie to become that liquor upon which
God imbibes, as He reels through space, an
eternity of blissful, drunken
swagger.

Year-end winds assault the house—so are
things tested in this world;
my maternal name is *Gale*—just like
Dorothy in Wizard of Oz: it's a
wind that blew me to this place, Earth;

it will be a wind that will carry me
Home again.
Neither a leaf in the air, nor a stolid
wall, I have learned this partnership well:
wings out strong, and the slightest

adjustments guide my trajectory.
Neither struggling nor resisting, Spirit and
I are partners in this ancient eloquent
dance. Balance, equilibrium, trust and
acceptance, and

all heights are possible.

I remember all my old lovers, and
what I loved most about
each;

harder to remember who left
whom—harder still to recall the
reasons.

Spring turns to summer, summer to
fall: why question the ways of
nature?

for Ruth:

Who knew that life could last so long?
It's been more than a half-century since
I held your hands.

Life is too short for some, and too
long for others—but who can say what is
lost or gained?

The paradox is that in time we abandon the
illusion of time, and we find that hands we
once held are still there in ours.

Somewhere in Heaven there is a small
café: let's steal away now—surely we have
paid our dues (if not earned our

ticket)—and meet there for tea, and the
Cuisine of the Masters!

NEVER lose track of the ones you
love, and if you do, spend the rest of your
life hunting them down!
Life is short, people frail, time treacherous and
relentless;

second chances are as rare as dragon
scales—the Ocean gives her pearls willingly, but
only in their season, and never
indiscriminately;

when a hand reaches forth, be not
shy, be not proud, be not
cavalier.

Who could have imagined that in my
dotage so many a handsome young
singer and composer would
transfigure my poems into such artful
sublimity—while I, the reclusive
bard, find my treasures in the
violets and the ferns upon my wee
speck of Terra Sacra?

Poetry grows from the earth and
like all good things seeks the eternal
Sun—that sparrows, sprites and
fauns find it along the way is both the
nature of art and the grace of the
Muse.

Like Blake, like Whitman, like
Dickinson, I find fodder in both
things seen and unseen, and the
music I hear seeps like honey from
voice, reed and instrument unfettered by
thought, tradition and
temporality.

To all who read my scribblings:
Thank you—you are the stars in an
eternal Sky, and the notes in a
symphony that was begun before the
world was set into spin!

There is a drunkenness that gin cannot alter,
there is a sobriety that requires bare feet and
laughter;
there is a craziness that stays the heart, and a
love that crushes mountains.

Here at Graybeard Abbey, the winter wind
sprouts up though cracks in the
floorboards, cats dominate furniture and
petition for more logs on the fire;

on a starry night, the mountains gleam silver
surrounding—
on a starless night there is a brightness that
obliterates shadows.

There is a peace that comes with cat on
lap and a book in hand,
and there is a peace that levels battlefields;
all I have is all I want,
and all I want is what I have—

the madness of the world stops at our
fence.
Sometimes, in the high poplars, the Moon may
perch for hours, flinging stars and
comets to the ground, while

denizens of the darkened forest pick up their
flutes and drums—
and neighbors sleep blissfully unaware.
Sometimes, the clock stops moving altogether,
and within that stillness

all becomes Perfectly Clear.

About GAVIN GEOFFREY DILLARD

Gavin Geoffrey Dillard bound his first collection of wisdom poems, couplets, and koans in 2nd grade. In 11th grade, at the North Carolina School of the Arts, his English professor, a regional poet, pulled him from class and spent the next two years tutoring him in poetry poetry poetry. In his senior year Gavin was flown to New York for the publishing of his first book, and spent time under the auspices of Ginsberg, Harold Norse, Ian Young, and other icons of the day. Dillard has published eight additional collections, two anthologies, and his infamous memoir, **In The Flesh *(undressing for success)*.** Branded by the Los Angeles Times "The Naked Poet" for his in-the-buff poetry readings, his poems have been recorded by James Earl Jones and published in anthologies and periodicals worldwide.

Gavin studied playwriting with Tom Eyen, Jerome Lawrence, and Robert Patrick. He has written comedy patter with and for Joan Rivers, Peggy Lee, Vincent Price, Lily Tomlin, and Dolly Parton. With Peter Allen he wrote a theme song for the LA Olympics. He wrote book and lyrics for **BARK!** *(the musical)*, which has played all over the Americas, and **OMFG!!!** *(an iLove story)*, which premiered in San Francisco in 2014; Gavin has written themes and jingles for Disney, Ralph Edwards Studios, and Chanticleer.

Two of Dillard's poems, set by Jake Heggie and recorded numerous times, were performed at Lincoln Center by Jennifer Larmore. Many classical art songs have ensued, and recently John de los Santos fashioned an opera entirely from Dillard's verse, composed by Clint Borzoni. Winning the prestigious Frontiers Award, **When Adonis Calls** premiered in 2015 at the Fort Worth Opera, followed by OPERA America's "best new work" award in 2017. Dillard's 3rd book, **Notes from a Marriage**, is regularly performed as a theatrical, and is currently being set as a solo opera.

Originally noted for his romantic-themed work, somewhere along the line, from a wee cabin on the foggy Marin cliffs, in the company of buddies Timothy Leary, Ram Das, and all the happening gurus of the hour, Dillard veered from the romantic back to his starting point of mystical metaphor.

Though a fan of spiritual poetry from every corner of the world, his principle influences remain the classics of early Taoism. He, however, claims both William Blake and Ono no Komachi as previous incarnations. Gavin lives with seven cats on a small tea plantation in Black Mountain, NC.

About the

GAVIN DILLARD POETRY LIBRARY & ARCHIVE

The Gavin Dillard Poetry Library & Archive, a not-for-profit charitable corporation, was created in 2016 to collect, promote, publish, and archive the writings of Gavin Geoffrey Dillard, working in tandem with the Gavin Dillard archives in the James C. Hormel LGBT Center of the San Francisco Public Library.

www.ingramcontent.com/pod-product-compliance
Lightning Source LLC
Chambersburg PA
CBHW021827090426
42811CB00032B/2055/J